The Search for ⊥ ⌐g

The Search for Enlightenment

An Introduction to Eighteenth-Century French Writing

John Leigh

Duckworth

First published in 1999 by
Gerald Duckworth & Co. Ltd.
61 Frith Street, London W1V 5TA
Tel: 0171 434 4242
Fax: 0171 434 4420
Email: enquiries@duckworth-publishers.co.uk

A catalogue record for this book is available
from the British Library

ISBN 0 7156 2839 9

Typeset by Derek Doyle & Associates
Mold, Flintshire
Printed in Great Britain by
Redwood Books Ltd, Trowbridge

Contents

Acknowledgements

I would like to thank those who stimulated my interest in eighteenth-century French literature and those who have encouraged me while writing this book: Marion Jeanneret, Michael Kempson, J. Patrick Lee, Jenny Mander, Michael Moriarty, Justin Meggitt, Jerry Toner, David Woodhouse and Melanie Wright. I wish to thank Robin Baird-Smith and Martin Rynja from Duckworth and above all Nick Hammond for his enlightened advice and friendship.

Author's Note

Detailed bibliographical references have been kept to a minimum in this book. Lists of secondary reading appear at the end of each chapter. All translations of French quotations are my own with the exception of: *Le Mondain*, taken from *The Works of M. de Voltaire*, ed. by Thomas Smollett (Dublin: R. Marchbank, 1772-73); *Lettres d'une Péruvienne*, taken from Letters from a *Peruvian Woman*, translated by David Kornacker (New York: MLA, 1993); Beaumarchais's plays, taken from *Beaumarchais, The Figaro Plays*, translated by John Wells (London: Dent, 1997).

Introduction

Between the death of Louis XIV in 1715 and the birth of a first
French Republic in 1792 a nation learned to see more clearly, to
dream more vividly, to laugh more freely, to groan more loudly.
Telescoped in this way, the years which carried France from one
state to the other, and the ferment of ideas with which they are
associated, are known as the vaunted Age of Reason, the 'siècle des
Lumières' or the Century of Enlightenment. These labels are at
once grand and derisory. They seem to flatter and not merely
cover the real age – like the magnificent wigs which adorn many
eighteenth-century portraits. And once we look beneath them,
they reveal, as wigs do, a different, not always attractive sight. It
then becomes clear that eighteenth-century French literature is
not only a vehicle for Enlightenment but a composite of movements which variously accompany and diverge from it.

An introduction to the literature of the eighteenth century, nevertheless, can barely overstate the importance of the century as a
nursery for many ideas, beliefs and assumptions that prevail in the
modern world. Perhaps the most emphatic statement of the ideals
of the Enlightenment, the monument *par excellence* to its ambitions,
the bible of its philosophers, is to be found in the voluminous
Encyclopédie, ou dictionnaire raisonné des sciences, des arts et des métiers,
(known more commonly as the *Encyclopédie*) published between
1751 and 1772 by a team orchestrated by Denis Diderot and Jean
le Rond d'Alembert. The articles and accompanying plates which
celebrate the intellectual and artisinal accomplishments of man
depict man understanding and living in harmony with the world
beyond. A hitherto elusive unity between man and the world
seemed to be promised and Diderot, in the entry 'Encyclopédie',
expresses the optimistic belief that knowledge might lead to virtue
which in turn would result in happiness, 'que nos neveux,

devenant plus instruits, deviennent en même temps plus vertueux et plus heureux' (that our descendants, becoming more educated, become at the same time more virtuous and happier).

These hopes and convictions still resonate now. However, weary hindsight has taught us to consider the eighteenth century as an age of great confidence. It is with as much pity as envy that we look upon these times when writers feel supremely assured in their capacity to improve their lot, to think on their own feet, to identify and to vilify enemies, to write and to be right. Make my enemies ridiculous, prayed the century's most feared satirist, Voltaire and, it has been acknowledged, his wish was in general granted to him. But there, nevertheless, remained serious enemies. Their continued, increasingly insidious presence means that enlightenment remains envisioned more than it is achieved, a process rather than a product. If the century's confident purposefulness impresses and inspires, its chief stimulus often seems to be frustration. The writers of the century not only have their own ideas about how to effect or enhance Enlightenment, but different visions of what that it itself might be. The Enlightenment can be considered as much the province of writers, whether dramatists or novelists, as theorists and scientists. In some cases these are the same people. The eighteenth century is the age of the last polymaths. The texts composed by these 'universal geniuses' encompass enquiries into philosophical and scientific matters as well as committing themselves to the forms of writing that we now know as literature. The boundaries between fiction and philosophy are indistinct, so that it is dangerous to detach and impose a distinctive, exalted category of 'literature' from the many activities of the Enlightenment. In the eighteenth century this term, both in French and English, refers to a general condition of intellectual refinement rather than to a specific corpus of texts. 'Littérature' tends to mean what might be called learning, or reading in the widest sense and, before specialisation and the division of knowledge into subjects, such reading envisages these subjects as a totality of interrelated exercises.

The Enlightenment is a pan-European phenomenon. In this unusually cosmopolitan age it is then not only difficult to talk specifically about 'literature' but to delineate the particular qualities of a French literature. The precepts of Neo-classicism, an art which characterises itself as of immutable and international value, holds sway for long periods in many quarters, particularly in France. Moreover, French writers not only travelled widely across Europe but, better still, themselves became tourist destinations. Voltaire's home in Ferney became *de rigueur* for those on the Grand Tour, while Rousseau's fame made his final resting place at Ermenonville a new European centre of pilgrimage. It is fair to say that many French writers enjoyed more in common with their foreign counterparts in the European Republic of letters than with their compatriots. Edward Gibbon wrote as effortlessly in French as Voltaire had done in English. The French take a particular pride in the fact that theirs is a universal language. Concomitantly, French identity is often perceived to result from language as well as location.

It is, nevertheless, helpful to inspect the particular problems and opportunities that confront French writers as well as writers of French. France was acknowledged to be politically retrograde in comparison to many of its rivals and yet a legacy of absolutism and intolerance coincides with an incomparable tradition in what is known as *belles lettres*, or the arts. Furthermore, writers in the eighteenth century are in many cases convinced that the French language is the clearest, most elegant and most supportive medium of the arts. Antoine Rivarol's exultant conclusion in his *Discours sur l'universalité de la langue française* that 'ce qui n'est pas clair n'est pas français' (that which is not clear is not French) rests on such a consensus well established by the beginning of the eighteenth century. In many centres of Europe, notably the courts of Berlin and St. Petersburg, it was the French language which sometimes gave expression to liberal ideas scorned in France. This tension seems to have been productive. It accounts for the sense that it was the responsibility of writers to change the world. Figaro, the indefatigable writer of seemingly inconsequential ballads in Beaumarchais's comedies, is a most sensitive and effective enemy of injustice. He acts by speaking and writing while Voltaire makes explicit their alliance when claiming in his correspondence: 'j'écris pour agir' (I write in order to act). French writers feel the *malaises* of the eighteenth century more acutely than many of their

European counterparts, but they also feel that they are the best equipped to carry the fight.

Although the polymath enjoys a prestige perhaps unknown since, this confidence is in many cases accompanied by a more precarious sense of what authors are and what their rights might be. Eighteenth-century French writers are not just united in a grand collective enterprise known as the Enlightenment, but there results from their efforts a new, precarious sense of the individual. The confidence apparently required to be a polymath is accompanied by a sense of responsibility towards others. It is both a source of self-doubt and self-congratulation that the genius becomes a more collective figure, a less pronounced individual who embraces the responsibilities to his society. Even those writers whose achievements were celebrated as extraordinary and unique were prepared to work on the collective projects of the age. The century developed increasingly collective ways of organising knowledge and reflection. Journals, such as the *Correspondance littéraire* edited over years by Frédéric-Melchior, baron de Grimm, exerted a new influence, while numerous provincial academies flourished in the course of the century.

It would be unwise to try to divorce texts from the ideas that are often their *raison d'être*. By the same token, however, ideas should not be lifted and isolated from the texts. It would be equally dangerous to try to summarise the century only by examining the ideas that animate it. It will be clear that the texts which are their vehicle need to be read and, as importantly, can be enjoyed. The Enlightenment teaches its adherents how to feel and introduces new ways of reading. Even in his sober *Discours préliminaire* which acts as a preface to the *Encyclopédie*, Jean le Rond d'Alembert argues that as well as propounding reason, people wish to communicate their passions:

> Les hommes en se communiquant leurs ideés, cherchent aussi à se communiquer leurs passions. C'est par l'éloquence qu'ils y parviennent. Faite pour parler au sentiment, comme la logique et la grammaire parlent à l'esprit, elle impose silence à la raison même;
>
> (In communicating to one another their ideas, people also seek to communicate to each other their passions. It is through eloquence

that they achieve this. Made to speak to our feelings, as logic and grammar speak to our intelligence, it imposes silence on reason itself.)

D'Alembert, who was himself celebrated as a geometer rather than a writer, suggests that, far from being antagonistic, ideas and passions may run in tandem and indeed that the passions may out-pace the ideas. He observes also that in this Age of Reason eloquence perhaps houses the ultimate power, a power which, frighteningly, can take reason itself hostage.

It must be emphasised that it is in writing and reading that the possibilities for Enlightenment were envisaged, but there too that the threats to it were in place. In writing texts, the authors of the Enlightenment were not just reflecting the ideas of the Enlightenment but reflecting on what it meant to be an author. This is the age in which author's rights, as well as the rights of man, were introduced. Until the late eighteenth century when, finally, an inchoate form of copyright was introduced, works did not belong so obviously to authors. The prefaces to many of these works remind us of the gap between the text which the author has written and the book which is read, of the traffic which blocks the route from one to the other. Severed from their authors, shifting between different pairs of hands, these works are pirated, revised and parodied at whim – as well, of course, as being misread.

Inured to piracy and pastiche, eighteenth-century authors and readers live with this *modus operandi* by installing a sense of the text as provisional, belonging to no-one and everyone. Authors seize the creative potential that obstruction provides by pre-emptively denying readers any sense of possession. Laclos's *Liaisons dangereuses*, with its two mutually exclusive prefaces explaining the text's provenance and purpose, is just one such example, while the Marquise de Merteuil's self-designed curriculum which she itemises in the *Liaisons dangereuses*, 'un chapitre de *Sopha*, une lettre d'Héloïse et deux contes de La Fontaine' (a chapter from *Le Sopha*, a scandalous novel by Crébillon *fils*, 1742), a letter from Héloïse (Rousseau's novel) and two tales from La Fontaine), is the ideal regime for a mind wishing to negotiate the conventions and gratify the tastes of that society. Eighteenth-century French society has a particular taste for the pithy expression. It prizes the decisive 'bon mot', the brief work which suggests insouciant versatility. The advice which Diderot, a fanatical enthusiast of Samuel Richardson's novels, dispenses to a French readership tried by their great length is possibly more facetious than pragmatic:

> Mes chers concitoyens, si les romans de Richardson vous paraissent longs, que ne les abrégez-vous? soyez conséquents. Vous n'allez guère à une tragédie que pour le dernier acte. Sautez tout de suite aux vingt dernières pages de *Clarisse.*

> (My dear fellow citizens, if the novels of Richardson seem too long to you, why don't you abridge them? Be consistent. You almost always go to watch a tragedy for the last act. Jump straightaway to the last twenty pages of *Clarissa.*)

Hopping between different authors and chopping particular texts, I aim to convey the sinuous characteristics of a century itself prone to such activities. This study will share Diderot's assumption when he remarks that the most important ideas are not those which have been sustained with an unwavering conviction but those to to which one returns repeatedly. This is then an attempt not so much at a history of ideas as a reading of them, as they are refracted in a number of texts. This study will try to show history, thought and text interacting in a way which does not do prejudice either to the importance of the idea in this age or the delights of reading its literature. If we acknowledge that the Enlightenment's influence is pervasive in eighteenth-century French literature this does not mean that its effects are uniform. Many writers committed to the Enlightenment question its impact and their own works are pulled in different directions. Unlike previous studies of this size, this one will show some of the doubts and anxieties that inform the writing of eighteenth-century French authors. It will argue that there is much more to the age than the rationalism, clarity and confidence with which it tends to be associated.

The eighteenth century saw more writing published than ever before and prodigious amounts were written by certain authors alone. This output is of a quality and quantity that remain frankly breathtaking. But the literature of the eighteenth century is also inexhaustible, for the simple reason that, as Borges said, a book itself is. The most exclusive chapters or trenchant categories are likely to look embarrassed when faced by particular works that may be read at once as novel or philosophy and reread as comedy or tragedy. A good number of eighteenth-century texts will need to be invited to the most select gathering of works or they will gatecrash it anyway.

Marivaux's 'indigent philosophe ou l'homme sans souci' (the destitute philosopher or the man without a care), the narrator of an essay of that name (1727), declares, with no scruple about the dignity of his philosophical text:

> Je veux qu'on trouve de tout dans mon livre, (je veux que les gens sérieux, les gais, les tristes, quelquefois les fous, enfin que tout le monde me cite) et vous verrez qu'on me citera.

> (I want you to find something of everything in my book, (I want the serious, the cheerful, the sad people, sometimes the mad people, in fact everyone to quote me) and you will see that I will be quoted.)

The 'indigent philosophe' is characteristic of his century in carrying off this curiously presumptuous modesty. He is characteristic also in articulating the desire for totality while accepting and inviting within that a selective, subjective reading – and he was right in saying that he would be quoted.

Selected Reading

Daniel Brewer, *The Discourse of Enlightenment in Eighteenth-Century France* (Cambridge: Cambridge University Press, 1993). With an emphasis on 'Diderot and the Encyclopedie', a study of the representation of knowledge in eighteenth-century France.

Norman Hampson, *The Enlightenment* (Harmondsworth: Penguin, 1968). A good introduction to the concepts and ambitions of the Enlightenment.

Leonard Kreiger, *Kings and Philosophers: 1689-1789* (Norton, 1970). A useful historical and political background.

Roy Porter, *The Enlightenment* (London: Macmillan, 1990). A helpful and interesting survey of the Enlightenment.

Daniel Roche, *France in the Enlightenment* (Cambridge MA: Harvard University Press, 1999). A study of politics and culture, institutions and people in the Enlightenment.

John W. Yolton, ed. *The Blackwell Companion to the Enlightenment* (Oxford: Oxford University Press, 1991). An excellent guide to the problems and preoccupations of the Enlightenment.

I

The Legacy of the Seventeenth Century

1. Seventeenth-Century Thinkers

After the heat of the *roi* soleil's brilliant regime the pallid light of the dawning Lumières was a relief. The reign of this *roi soleil*, the Sun King, Louis XIV (1643-1715), endowed to those who had experienced it ambivalent memories of a uniquely impressive civilisation and a painfully oppressive regime. Transfixed by this age in all its aspects, the thinkers of a century rolling inexorably towards the Revolution may appear curiously retrospective. But if the eighteenth century is a nursery of ideas, the seventeenth century was their birthplace. A history of eighteenth-century thought must also be a history of the seventeenth century. Never, in recent times, had a century been so dazzled by the previous one and so conscious of its own pallor. Even the most independent minds of the eighteenth century were impressed with the brilliance and the originality of the thinkers and writers of the previous century. But this reverence always, if tacitly, acts as a commentary on their own age, a self-assessment exercise. The debt to seventeenth-century thought and literature can be measured not only in sounding authors for the widespread sense of decline they feel but in appreciating the way these very losses could be rehabilitated as gains. It is by excavating the previous century that the writers of the eighteenth century appreciate better both their own deficiencies and their good fortune.

Born in 1694, Voltaire is the author most responsible for guiding the eighteenth century out of the seventeenth, for giving it new directions while embodying its propensity to look back. Like many of his contemporaries, Voltaire often appreciated the methods of his illustrious predecessors without approving of the conclusions to which those methods led. Of the seventeenth-century philosophical expositions, René Descartes's methodical doubt, his attempt to penetrate to clear and distinct ideas outlined in his *Discours de la méthode*, was highly influential in providing an example for philosophers of the courage and independence required to distil into clear, abstract formulations the complexities of philosophy. The eighteenth century inherits from Descartes his affirmation of human freedom and his belief in the mastery and autonomy of the human spirit. But Descartes's ideas about matter and the mind, the division of body and soul, were, however influential, contested, as the century rejected systematism in favour of empiricism and sought truths that were verifiable in experience. Descartes's understanding of animals as machines provided the platform for subsequent radical visions of man as a soulless, mechanical entity. Such ideas would be the basis for the speculative, scientific exposition, *L'Homme machine*, published by Julien Offray de La Mettrie, a doctor at the court of Frederick the Great, in 1748, which argued that man, without a soul, could be understood to function as a machine. They percolate also into the writings and observations of Choderlos de Laclos and the Marquis de Sade whose characters are frequently propelled and ruled by such mechanical operations. In rejecting this dualism of body and soul, matter and thought, to accommodate a vision of a world that was not divided but transforming, Diderot, like other eighteenth-century thinkers, finds the stimulus in the work of another great seventeenth-century rationalist, the *Ethics* of Baruch Spinoza (1632-77). Spinoza had argued, through the use of geometrically ordered propositions, that God was impersonal rather than the anthropomorphic Judaeo-Christian God of the Bible and substituted for him an all-embracing concept of God that seemed to make him identical to and therefore inseparable from nature. His watchword 'Deus sive Natura' (God or Nature) echoed through the eighteenth century. It appealed to the many eighteenth-century philosophers inclined to locate ultimate truth in nature rather than in scriptural authority and convinced that creator and creation were not distinct but the same.

Descartes, whose ideas had won acceptance in France only after a long struggle was himself duly challenged and, largely through the work of John Locke in his *Essay Concerning Human Understanding* (1690), a new theory of human psychology unfolded. Locke refuted the view that certain ideas were innate to man, maintaining instead that man was like a blank sheet of paper on which experience and sense-impressions left their imprint. Like Spinoza's writings, Locke's works helped the eighteenth century to conceive new ideas in relation to the tortuous questions of mind and matter. But the figure that both gave the century its confidence to embark on new philosophical journeys and haunted it by its failure to produce a thinker of comparable genius, was Isaac Newton (1642-1727). Voltaire, who later published the *Éléments de la philosophie de Newton* and whose mistress, the Marquise du Châtelet, translated the *Principia*, was concerned to introduce the ideas of Newton, convinced that his insights would advance French thought and temper fanaticism. Voltaire is remarkable in introducing complex scientific ideas in a vocabulary and imagery seemingly at odds with them. In the sixteenth of the *Lettres philosophiques* (first published in English as the *Letters upon the English Nation* (1733), Newton is announced in messianic terms. Voltaire stages a sort of annunciation in which the truth is revealed prophetically and directly to Descartes:

> ... et il viendra un homme qui démontrera ces paradoxes, et qui anatomisera un seul rayon de lumière avec plus de dextérité que le plus habile artiste ne dissèque le corps humain. Cet homme est venu.

> (and there will come a man who will demonstrate these paradoxes and who will anatomise a single ray of light with more dexterity than the most skilful artist can dissect the human body. This man has come.)

The language of metaphysics is enlisted to understand his physics. Newton's demonstration that miracles are scientific is itself miraculous. Earlier, in the first letter of the *Lettres philosophiques*, Voltaire had quoted John the Baptist's prophecy 'mais un autre viendra après moi', a paraphrase of John XIV, 2 'I go to prepare a place for you'. In much the same way as John the Baptist prepares for and announces the Messiah, so Descartes prepares for Newton. Newton is a hero worthy of the Enlightenment in that he understands light itself. He instils confidence that man will be able to illuminate other spheres. The co-ordinates he had pinned down might, it was hoped, be available in other areas of intellectual endeavour. Voltaire preaches the truth of Newton's philosophy and, by extending the jurisdiction of the religious vocabulary, weakens its claims to exclusive rights over the truth.

The thunderbolt of Newton's advent recalls the famous hemistich (the term for six syllables of verse or half an alexandrine, the stateliest form of classical verse) of Boileau in his *Art poétique* (1674), which announces the arrival of François de Malherbe (1555-1628) and the birth of true French writing: 'Enfin Malherbe vint' (At last Malherbe came). The great man's arrival is described in similarly spectacular terms. Descartes's *tabula rasa*, the clean slate with which he had started, Newton's advent or even Peter the Great's construction of a capital city were privileged because they represented supreme creations *ex nihilo* (out of nothing) and so they won the pained envy of an age which knew that 'tout est dit' (everything has been said), and that even that had already been said.

This constellation of figures and references left many eighteenth-century writers numb. The 'querelle' between the 'anciens' and the 'modernes' (the quarrel between the ancients and the moderns) which had divided and excited seventeenth-century thinkers remained central, as Madame Dacier and Houdart de la Motte took the baton from Fontenelle and Perrault in arguing about translations of Homer. Classical texts and figures remained absolutely central to the understanding and discussion of contemporary questions, but, perhaps aided by the discovery and exploration of the ruins of Herculaneum and Pompeii in 1738 and 1748, there was a particular fascination with decline. But it was no longer to the Ancients and to the Mediterranean south that France looked chiefly, but, horror of horrors, to that 'natural and necessary enemy of hers, England. If eighteenth-century France was entranced by the seventeenth century it innovated by turning its attention northwards to the English seventeenth century and contemporary thought and writing. Voltaire's *Lettres philosophiques* shifts the emphasis to England by paying attention not only to the thought of Locke, Newton and Shaftesbury but by popularising in, when not introducing to, France the works of Pope and Shakespeare. The achievements of these writers, like those of Lawrence Sterne and Samuel Richardson which would be applauded as much as thought and philosophy, also ushered in the 'Anglomanie' which swept through France in the eighteenth century, as its writers tried out new ways of feeling as well as thinking. English gardens were ultimately as influential as the English philosophers who walked in them.

2. Seventeenth-Century Writers

In 1727 Voltaire attended the funeral of Newton in St. Paul's Cathedral. But he comes not only to praise Newton, he comes to bury him. In lavishing praise on him and the century to which he belonged, Voltaire intimates a sense that this era is to be followed by a less spectacular age. He catalogues the most eminent seventeenth-century authors at the end of his history of the previous century, *Le Siècle de Louis XIV* (published fully first in 1751). Characteristic of the eighteenth-century desire to collate and order, it was and, in some cases, remains seminal in acting as a 'Who's Who' for seventeenth-century French culture. In affirming this order he also seals it, entombing the authors of the great age in a new canon. He attends their burial too. If the eighteenth century could profit from and refine the thought of the seventeenth-century thinkers, the masterpieces of the theatre held their successors in thrall. These works are as important to the consciousness of the eighteenth century. It has been observed that Descartes's revolutionary method coincides with the new view of the world embodied by Miguel de Cervantes's *Don Quixote*, published in Spain in 1605 and 1615, but if science and thought were moving in a steadily upward trajectory, the course the arts were taking remained at best unpredictable and, at worst, impoverished precisely because of the attention these other spheres of knowledge was attracting.

The plays of Molière, Racine and Corneille were seen as the

cream of seventeenth-century writing. They represented the acme of a civilisation that had reached unparalleled heights under Louis XIV. When, in 1760, Marie Françoise Corneille, the impoverished great-niece of the renowned Pierre Corneille, came to Voltaire's notice, he set about raising money for her by selling subscriptions to his study of Corneille's writings, the *Commentaires sur Corneille* (completed in 1764). The reverence which eighteenth-century authors felt for their predecessors was coloured poignantly by a sense of the poverty and abeyance into which genius and its legacy had fallen. But it must be rescued by social beneficence rather than emulated by literary genius. In a similar vein the eponymous nephew of Diderot's provocative dialogue, *Le Neveu de Rameau* (begun *c.*1760), the agonised descendant of a genius (the great composer Jean-Philippe Rameau, 1683-1764) finds solace in the allegation that Racine, genius that he is, was no saint. This may help him to accept the inferiority of his own branch or 'rameau' of the Rameau family tree. A discussion ensues in which Rameau's nephew and his interlocutor argue whether the mediocre but reasonable citizen is preferable to the talented but wayward artist. We can, argues one of the interlocutors, forgive ourselves the failure to produce a Racine with the assurance that we are socially more acceptable. In turn this discussion voices questions about whether society should be propitious to genius or favourable to decency or can be both.

Genius does what it must, and Talent does what it can, so it has been said. The writers of the eighteenth century dislike despotism, even that of genius, and are prepared to accept mediocrity by qualifying it as egalitarian. Aesthetic questions are thus often relativised by their causes and effects in society. There is then a consensual admiration of the achievement of the eighteenth-century greats, but it is clear that that appreciation itself rests on new grounds and responds to a new aesthetic and that the age characteristically will make an opportunity of its *malaise*.

3. The Eighteenth-Century Self-Image

While the eighteenth century tries to forge connections between different, apparently discrete areas, its abiding belief that these areas are interrelated, even interdependent, can also inhibit. Progress in one area is sometimes held to be purchased at the price of neglect in other areas, and writers such as Diderot are quick to explore the implications for society and ordinary people of the conclusions to which abstract philosophy comes. If art is regarded as an opportunity for mediating new ideas and venting new possibilities, there remains an anxiety that in committing itself only to didactic ends, it will lose its value. The torpor of poetry in the century is often attributed to the pervasive influence of geometry. In his *Discours préliminaire* to the *Encyclopédie* it is perhaps with some guilt that d'Alembert observes:

> Notre siècle porté à la combinaison et à l'analyse, semble vouloir introduire les discussions froides et didactiques dans les choses de sentiment [...] Cette anatomie de l'âme s'est glissée jusque dans nos conversations; on y disserte, on n'y parle plus; et nos sociétés ont perdu leurs précieux agréments, la chaleur et la gaieté.

> (Our century disposed to combination and analysis seems to want to introduce cold and didactic discussions into matters of sentiment [...] This anatomy of the soul has slipped into our conversations in which we no longer talk but hold forth; and our societies have lost their precious charms, their warmth and gaiety.)

However, even the century's self-satisfied sense of its analytic and critical prowess could be disturbed. It was also observed that a penchant for ridicule threatened the serious endeavour of thinkers, whether in historical, scientific or textual matters, since pedantry was widely considered the greatest sin. 'On effleure tout, on n'approfondit rien' (we skim over everything and don't think hard about anything), says Bordeu in *Le Rêve de d'Alembert* with an incalculable mixture of satisfaction and contrition. The articles 'Ridicule' and 'Littérature' in the *Encyclopédie* regret that this fear of pedantry had cost progress and success in the literature of the period. This view seems at odds with d'Alembert's observation in its preface that chilly didactic seminars had supplanted animated discussions. If the thinkers could satisfy themselves that theirs was an age of levity and spirit, it disturbed many of them that it seemed incapable of the sustained intensity and gravitas which was the true grandeur of the previous century. The two views cannot be reconciled and neither view is shared by all thinkers in the eighteenth century. Indeed this is the very charge levelled at their contemporaries by some writers in post-Revolutionary France who were inclined to admire nostalgically the supremacy of wit and conversation under the ancien regime. The contrasting observations, nevertheless, share a common fascination in the damage to an area which may be entailed by progress in another, whether this means investigating the extent to which philosophy might injure morality, or the theatre could harm society, or conversation may endanger or be endangered by science.

D'Alembert goes on in the following lines of his *Discours* to observe that the ages of Demosthenes and Virgil were succeeded by mediocrity, and he lists some of the authors who exemplify it. The detail of the example provides not only historical evidence but in itself a present instance of the tendency to dry, analytical, anatomical dissertation. The interest in history which developed throughout the century was considered, even by some of its exponents, to be the index of an age disposed to considering previous centuries rather than asserting the qualities of its own. Even those satisfied that this was an age more reasonable than any of its barbaric predecessors could not help looking back with wistful retrospection. In the eighteenth century history is often designed to validate the present but it also can gratify nostalgia. Like Edward Gibbon, Montesquieu is fascinated by decline. His *Considérations sur les causes de la grandeur des Romains et de leur décadence* (Considerations on the causes of the grandeur and the decline of the Romans) was published in 1734, over forty years before *The History of the Decline and Fall of the Roman Empire.* Voltaire voices these fears of decline with all the simplicity and sadness of a certainty: 'on a beaucoup écrit dans ce siècle; on avait du génie dans l'autre' (much has been written in this century; they had genius in the previous one). In the *Siècle de Louis XIV*, Voltaire views the seventeenth century as an age of genius which has been succeeded by an age of critique. Although the history was carefully written to reflect a mixture of appreciation and criticism, it was deplored as an implicit critique of Louis XV. The authorities were conscious that praise for the previous century amounted to a deprecation of their own. They were perhaps disconcerted by the decision to conclude the history with a discussion of seemingly recondite disputes about ceremonies in China. This unlikely move has the effect of suggesting that there were realms which reached beyond Louis XIV's jurisdiction and remained indifferent to his values and influences. But, more disturbingly, China also represents a paradigm for a nation that reached Enlightenment early, perhaps too early and, frozen on this lofty plateau, could not make good the progress it promised. Both these senses characterise the eighteenth century's self-definition when looking upon other ages. Any complacency that the age had achieved a measure of enlightenment after the rigours of the previous century is tempered by the sense that it now had nowhere to go.

After the death of Louis XIV new forms of authority were demanded by the eighteenth century. A new, different sort of father figure was created. The bestselling text of the early century was *Télémaque* (written *c.*1695) by Fénelon, a prose epic that seemed to align itself securely within the Classical tradition, by taking up a subject suggested by Homer's *Odyssey*. Télémaque's search for his father possibly corresponds to this desire for a new model of statesmanship. The advice dispensed by Mentor to his young protégé about the ideal state was perceived to be a critique of Louis XIV whose reign was drawing to an end. It earned Fénelon exile and disgrace. But many texts banished the father figure completely. Bastards abound in the fictions of the eighteenth century (Lesage's Gil Blas, Candide, Beaumarchais's Figaro as well as Chérubin's son Léon and Florestine his wife, the eponymous 'fils naturel' of Diderot's drama, to name but a few, are all illegitimate children), perhaps also an indication of the century's ambivalence about its own filiation as well as the embodiment of the ambiguities in the relations of society and nature which they throw up. Figaro finds his parents but finds that they are not only not the aristocrats he had envisaged but that they are not worthy of him. A dream of the nobility of one's past is overcome by a more meritocratic, sensible present.

The age's ambivalent feelings in front of the great century before are perhaps translated by this recurrent motif of the child which, removed from the jurisdiction of an unreasonable authority, totteringly finds its feet. Eventually the age locates its values in the sentimental space of the bourgeois family. Aided by Jean-Baptiste Greuze (1725-1805) and other painters of domestic scenes, the model of the good father, like that of the good mother, gains in stature. The sanctified transcendental authority of the Father is gradually eclipsed by that of the father relocated in the family, while later under the Revolution, the State presents itself as the Father. Jean-François Marmontel's posthumously published *Mémoires* (1792-94), dedicated to his children, seem to answer Rousseau's *Confessions*. Rousseau, who recommended in *Emile* that children should be removed from their families to maximise their educational potential, had achieved notoriety for giving his own children away. This was perhaps another way of starting afresh. In its adolescence the century rebelled against but admired the patriarchal power there of which it was neither fond nor capable. Before the eigheenth century itself tries on its own terms to become a good father, it had to shake off its allegiances to its own literary forefathers.

Eighteenth-century writers then encounter in their scrutiny of seventeenth-century works pervasive reminders of their own mediocrity. An interest in deficiency and impotence is characteristic of many eighteenth-century writers. In the wake of the *Grand siècle* (as the seventeenth century became known) they ask themselves what impotent man might say to us. This anxiety finds expression in motifs and images that stretch across different periods and different texts. Montesquieu's *Lettres persanes* depicts eunuchs in a collapsing absolutist regime, while Voltaire's Candide expresses dismay that, in eighteenth-century opera, *castrati* get to sing the parts of great Roman emperors. This seems to typify the emasculation that was widely thought to characterise eighteenth-century mores. Diderot, whose *Neveu de Rameau* is said to lack the usual elements that make up a man, wrote a text, the *Lettre sur les aveugles*, with the provocative subtitle 'à l'usage de ceux qui voient' (for the use of those who can see).

The blind, aged beggar Belisarius is a figure in the same idiom. A victorious general who had been instrumental in reviving the fortunes of the Roman Empire in the sixth century (when its

1. Jean-Baptiste Greuze, *The Well-Beloved Mother*, 1769. © Marquis de Laborde Collection, Madrid.

2. Jean-Baptiste Greuze, *A Lady Reading the Letters of Heloise and Abelard,* 1758-9.
© The Art Institute of Chicago, Chicago.

power base had moved to Byzantium), the wheel of fortune then turned spectacularly to his disadvantage. He was incriminated and blinded by the Emperor Justinian and left, impoverished, on the streets. Belisarius embodies this ambivalent sense of the infirmity of greatness which so troubles the eighteenth century. Jacques-Louis David was one of several painters attracted by the subject. His painting *Bélisaire demandant l'aumône* (*Belisarius receiving alms*), pictured on the front cover, was exhibited in 1781 to great acclaim. Diderot exclaimed in the *Salons* that he saw it every day and always thought that he was seeing it for the first time. David is especially adept in provoking different possible responses to the subject, and it would be invidious to view it only as the index of a self-conscious preoccupation with the characteristics of the age. Nevertheless, because, anachronistically, a Byzantine general is placed in an archetypally Classical context, it is possible to argue that the painting of Belisarius is not simply to be understood as a historiographical exercise. In neither the influential work of political theory by Jean-Francois Marmontel, *Bélisaire*, (written in 1765) where the blinded but wise old man advises a young man, Tibère, on statesmanship, much as Mentor had taught Télémaque in Fénelon's work, nor in the historical romance *Bélisaire* (1805), by Madame de Genlis, which, conversely, is designed to amuse 'les loisirs des femmes et des gens du monde' (the leisure of women and people in society), is the historical element foremost. These dual aspects suggested by Belisarius, the didactic, political message of the story and its sentimental dimension, widely characteristic of the century, are to be found here in David's painting.

The name of Belisarius was, the *Correspondance littéraire* (a journal which responded to the intellectual and artistic issues of the day and itself published original works) reports, 'consacré dans nos écoles à retracer à la jeunesse les vicissitudes de la bonne et et de la mauvaise fortune' (devoted in our schools to reminding young people of the vicissitudes of fortune) and, from the Roman philosopher Seneca onwards, teaches this stoical truth. Belisarius reminds the eighteenth century more specifically of the cruelty of arbitrary justice and the perils of despotism. The affront that the state had exercised power arbitrarily and let down one of its defenders was felt as keenly as the blow of capricious fortune.

Indeed the painting was perceived in some quarters to be a tacit commentary on the fate endured by the comte de Lally, a soldier in the victorious French army at Fontenoy in 1745, who was later unjustly accused of treason, executed in 1766, rehabilitated in 1778 and found guilty once again in 1784.

David, who was to become both an iconographer of the Revolution and the painter of Napoleon's imperial glory, places a dual emphasis on the impact of injustice and the dignity of grandeur. In his painting, the noble faces evoke emotion and consternation, but the hands are equally expressive here and their actions militate against any passivity in the face of anguish. The raised hands of the soldier indicate that force is suspended in recognition of respect, the imploring hands of the child and the delicate posture of the woman suggest that beneficence can rescue fallen grandeur and compassion compensate for injustice. Charity and compassion indifferent to age and fortune are emphasised here in a manner that typifies the eighteenth-century quest for a morality without Christianity. The painting has been viewed as a turning point in French art, as it heralds neo-Classicism. Although it is painted in subdued, sober colours, and the classical landscape recalls those of Nicolas Poussin, the picture still operates within the emotional conventions which prevailed earlier in the century. This coincidence of sentimentality and heroism, the paradox of weak grandeur or of clairvoyant blindness, haunts eighteenth-century French culture as it no doubt intrigued Diderot in the *Salon*.

David's painting may have suggested, on at least one of the occasions on which Diderot looked at it, that beneficence becomes the model not just to abet, but in fact to replace genius. In the neglect and absence of genius, the century sees itself as impoverished, but, nevertheless, rich in important, compensatory ways. The painting projects the union of different generations through sentiment and compassion even if, as the alarmed soldier who recognises the former general realises, the present is quite different from the past. Entertaining images of itself as an ailing grey-haired man who, toiling under injustice, lives off memories of grandeur and as a young, earnest figure keen to solicit support and encourage beneficence, the eighteenth century is at once Belisarius and the child.

Belisarius reminds the century of the fragility of man, even the great man, and the difficulty of achieving happiness in a cruelly unpredictable world. Nevertheless, where French seventeenth-century writers had seen man as subject not only to injustice but vulnerable to his own passions, their eighteenth-century counterparts looked more kindly on human nature and believed earnestly that man had a right to happiness.

Selected Reading

W. Doyle, *The Ancien Regime* (London: Macmillan, 1986). An overview of seventeenth- and eighteenth-century life in France.

Nicholas Hammond, *Creative Tensions: An Introduction to Seventeenth-Century French Literature* (London: Duckworth, 1997). An introduction that answers prejudices about seventeenth-century literature and suggests new approaches.

Ross Hutchison, *Locke in France, 1688-1734* (Oxford: Voltaire Foundation, 1991). The definitive study of the influences exerted on French writers by Locke.

A.C. Kors and P. Korshin, eds, *Anticipations of the Enlightenment* (Princeton: Princeton University Press, 1987). A study of the major pre-Enlightenment figures.

Peter A. Schouls, *Descartes and the Enlightenment* (Edinburgh: Edinburgh University Press, 1989). Lucid and interesting study of the Enlightenment's appropriation of Descartes.

II

In Search of Happiness

'Eh bien ne voilà-t-il pas encore un cependant?' (Well then, not yet another 'however'?) moans Silvia in Marivaux's comedy, *La Double inconstance* (1723). A critic of eighteenth-century literature must, however, be allowed to say 'however' or 'although' occasionally. Contradictions risk mocking our deductions or conclusions. Although the century sees itself impoverished it thinks itself rich; although it is wretched it is, however, self-satisfied – often if only because the causes of its misery were so identifiable.

So while Voltaire describes the century as a tottering bankrupt old man, France in the eighteenth century is in the literal sense, nevertheless, wealthier than it had been. Louis XIV's death had induced a collective sigh of relief and the Regency (1715-1723) which followed, under the sybaritic Philippe d'Orléans, Louis XIV's brother, ushered in a new age of pleasure. It is also clear that, beleaguered as they were by the censorious forces of absolutism, French writers still considered themselves privileged. A good number of eighteenth-century writers refer to the century in which they live as 'un siècle aussi heureux que le nôtre' (a century as fortunate as our own). Increased prosperity brought increased literacy. Reading was not only itself a pleasure hitherto denied to many people, but whether in song or verse, novel or play, readers were encouraged to seek further pleasure and assured that they deserved it.

Such insights were not as self-evident as they may now appear. In order to achieve them, powerful seventeenth-century traditions once again needed to be negotiated. The complex of religious ideas, which will be discussed in more detail later, suggested that happiness on earth was only to be found in the striving for the true and eternal felicity that lay beyond this earth. Blaise Pascal's exquisitely gloomy vision of man's place in the world and his distrust of our capacity to achieve a meaningful happiness represented yet a formidable obstacle. These views rested on the Pascalian conviction that 'le moi est haïssable' (the self is detestable). Many influential French writers of the previous century concurred that the assertion of the self as heroic was merely a loathsome form of self-preservation or self-delusion. Their eighteenth-century counterparts in general reject such self-loathing in favour of a more optimistic view of human nature. Self-interest is now deemed to be harmless and indeed salutary. However, many writers first find in a more distant past the gratification they do not dare to seek in their present.

Some eighteenth-century authors try to bypass Christian preoccupations by appealing to a warmer, Edenic past and they find in the history and writings of Roman and Greek times not only a source for polemical, political questions (as embodied by Telemachus or Belisarius) but the solace of pastoral and mythological stories. The sensuality in such tales is legitimised to an extent by their antiquity. The eighteenth century derived from the previous century its classical precepts but also its fondness for the pastoral life. It is rather surprising to see such thinkers as Montesquieu and Rousseau begin their careers with the gentle, anodyne *Temple de Gnide* (1725) or, in the latter case, the innocuously pastoral opera, *Le Devin du village* (1752). They may have been interpreted as interesting *post factum*, but it is safe to say that little in these texts indicates the philosophical stature their authors would later achieve. Both authors would also subsequently depict relationships between men and women in less comfortable terms.

Voltaire, who had already taken on Pascal in the *Lettres philosophiques*, can be relied upon to use blasphemous terms when urging man to gratify himself in the present. But he is equally concerned to discard the pastoral, mythological dreams of lost happiness which remain widely available in the century. These chimeras are dismissed as ineffectual and obstructive to proper happiness. Transfixed as he is by the genius of the previous century, Voltaire looks for happiness resolutely in his own age.

1. Voltaire, *Le Mondain* (1736)

Voltaire had established himself as the great epic poet which France had been wanting with *La Henriade*, which (published in 1724) preached the ecumenical virtues of Henri IV. In contrast *Le Mondain*, published in 1736, seems frivolous. The 'mondain' is someone who likes and belongs in the 'monde', a creature whose tastes are worldly and profane. This jolly poem, urging enjoyment of the present and indulgence of its plenty and prosperity epitomises a new spirit of licence. Cheekily, Voltaire opposes the austerity of religion with the abundance of a world profiting from commerce, but he is also concerned to attack any other form of reminiscence about 'the good old days':

> Regrettera qui veut le bon vieux temps,
> Et l'âge d'or, et le règne d'Astrée,
> Et les beaux jours de Saturne et de Rhée,
> Et le jardin de nos premiers parents;
> Moi, je rends grâce à la nature sage
> Qui, pour mon bien, m'a fait naître en cet age
> Tant décrié par nos tristes frondeurs:
> Ce temps profane est tout fait pour mes moeurs,
> J'aime le luxe, et même la mollesse,
> Tous les plaisirs, les arts de toute espèce,
> [...]
> O le bon temps que ce siècle de fer!
> Le superflu, chose très nécessaire
> A réuni l'un et l'autre hemisphère.
> Voyez-vous pas ces agiles vaisseaux
> Qui, du Texel, de Londres, de Bordeaux,
> S'en vont chercher, par un heureux échange,
> De nouveaux biens, nés aux sources du Gange,
> Tandis qu'au loin, vainqueurs des musulmans,
> Nos vins de France enivrent les sultans?

> Others may with regret complain,
> That 'tis not fair Astrea's reign,
> That the famed golden age is o'er

That Saturn, Rhea, rule no more:
Or, to speak in another style,
That Eden's groves no longer smile.
For my part, I thank nature sage,
That she has placed me in this age:
Religionists may rail in vain;
I own, I like this age profane;
I love the pleasures of a court;
I love the arts of every sort;
[...]
This iron age brings happy days.
Needful superfluous things appear;
They have joined together either sphere.
See how that fleet, with canvas wings,
From Texel, Bordeaux, London brings,
By happy commerce, to our shores
All Indus, and all Ganges stores;
Whilst France, that pierced the Turkish lines,
Sultans make drunk with rich French wines.

The various past times construed nostalgically as happy are chained together emphatically by the conjunction 'et' which, looming large at the beginning of the poem, invites us to move restlessly from one apparently happy moment to the next. The prominent 'et' lends to the beginning of the poem the quality of an inventory and this list emphasises that none of its items is perfect. There are simply too many of these perfect old times to be plausible. *L'Astrée*, the pastoral novel by Honoré D'Urfé (published 1607-27), the mythological figures of Saturn and Rhea, and, lumped in irreverently with these fictions, the story of Genesis, represent misguided attempts at locating happiness and, at worst, induce self-reproach and self-denial in the present.

Opposed to this indiscriminate assemblage of illusory *topoi* (or commonplaces) is the poet's call to look around quite simply and appreciate the visible, real benefits of commerce. He looks not back to an age from which we are fallen but forward to increased prosperity, convinced that man relies on civilisation and conversation to protect us from the ravages of nature and contrasting the misery of wild man with the happiness which arts and industry afford us. This 'Mondain' tells the reader to call off the search for transcendent felicity in the interests of profiting from the terrestrial paradise. The poem ends impudently as Voltaire proclaims 'le paradis terrestre est où je suis' (the terrestrial paradise is where I am). This paradise is not serene, but, prefiguring Candide's final imperative 'il faut cultiver notre jardin' (we must cultivate our garden), this Eden needs to be constantly landscaped according to our changing needs and wishes. This paradise differs from many others before and since by acknowledging the benefit, indeed the necessity to it, of money. Voltaire is one of a number of eighteenth-century figures who advocate luxury as a means of supporting society and assuring peace. These ideas, like the commerce they recommend, are exchanged all across Europe. Bernard Mandeville's *Fable of the Bees* (1714;1723), published repeatedly all over Europe, is perhaps the most influential work in outlining why 'luxury' is morally defensible and socially desirable. It provided many of the social and political arguments that lend weight to this imagery. The role of money in shaping society and the happiness of its members becomes central to the fictional and philosophical writings of the century. Whether good or bad, money was everywhere. The *Neveu de Rameau* makes this emphatically clear: 'De l'or, de l'or, l'or est tout; et le reste, sans or, n'est rien' (money, money, money is everything; and the rest, without money, is nothing).

The role of money in literature is in some cases traditional and predictable. Alain-René Lesage's comedy *Turcaret*, first performed in 1709, in the tradition of Molière's *Le Bourgeois gentilhomme*, is a satire of financiers and *parvenus*, promoted by his money beyond his station. However, such themes are increasingly refined and qualified by the sensibilities of such writers as Michel-Jean Sedaine, whose successful businessman/philosopher, Vanderk, renounces his aristocratic credentials because as a businessman he gains, in all senses, more credit. But in the period of the Regency, the coincidence of poverty and wealth is rendered more ambivalent by the notorious 'system' of John Law (1671-1729), the controller-general of French finance instrumental in introducing paper money which immediately loses it value. Money is increasingly responsible for a less determinate set of values which float with changing prices. The wider distribution of money creates a new fluidity in relationships between individuals. The once hapless Candide for instance donates some money to one of the dethroned monarchs he encounters towards the end of the *conte*, as money subverts the traditional hierarchies. But, equally, Des Grieux's story which the narrator has paid to hear in the Regency novel, *Manon Lescaut*, shows that the ubiquitous presence of money in society was reponsible for the degeneration of all kinds of relationships into transactions.

Voltaire's poem tells us different things about the century. Perhaps most importantly, he tries to tell the century that what it reads is at odds with what it should be feeling and doing. It is stuck with fairytales and pastoral stories that mislead it. *Le Mondain* attempts to substitute itself for such works. The poem is characteristic of the willingness of eighteenth-century writers to deploy readable forms in the service of ideas. Like Mandeville, Voltaire writes in verse rather than in the prose of a treatise. But the poem is not only readable. Its form embodies and renders plausible the central paradox: 'le superflu chose très nécessaire' (the superfluous is very necessary). As a poem it is undoubtedly and beautifully superfluous. It does not take the most economical route but exhibits its own artifice, its own shameless superfluity. The verse has a gratuitous, profligate savour. It is a self-consciously artificial product that takes pleasure in what it says. Yet a necessity also governs the form. The poet respects and celebrates the dictates of rhyme and rhythm here. The couplet demands and receives a rhyme while the regular rhythm of the poem lends the aura of inevitability that can characterise poetry. Form and content legitimise one another. A poem about luxury suits Voltaire's purposes better than a treatise on the subject since the paradox of superfluity and necessity is not only noted but actually experienced.

The insouciance of the poem masks and therefore permits importunate philosophical and social claims. Voltaire's apparently ingenuous credo barely disguises an urgent agenda. It was going to be impossible to seek something as important as happiness without colliding into the beliefs enshrined by authority and tradition. Inevitably, if almost imperceptibly, the taste for pastoral scenes duly gives way to a more dangerous form of hedonism, and the search for happiness then takes the eighteenth century down new, winding roads. In the earlier part of the eighteenth century the movement known as the Rococo, which encompasses all forms of art, gives expression to these new tastes. The *Fêtes galantes* of Antoine Watteau (1684-1721) and the genre paintings of François Boucher (1703-1770) and Jean-Honoré Fragonard (1732-1806) capture the delights of youth in exquisite, sensuous colours. This vogue for the inconsequential encounter and its transient pleasures answers the rubric known as the *vanités*, which placed a moralistic emphasis on the transience of human life. Where the latter sought to illustrate the truths of *Ecclesiastes* (a book in the Hebrew scriptures famous for declaring 'Vanity of vanities! All is vanity.') with their emblems of candles, hourglasses and bubbles, these genre paintings, which have no exact counterparts in the rest of Europe, tend to regard transience as a source of delight and joy.

In many of these genre paintings the innocent joys of freedom and youth are clouded by the threat of a burgeoning sexuality. They are prurient as well as pretty. They engage the viewer in an encounter with an episode or a figure that titillates or unsettles. Later in the century there would be a recoil from these pictures in the interest of a more morally dependable art. When, in 1771, Fragonard's series of paintings, known as *Les Progrès de l'amour* (The Progress of Love), destined for the palace of a former mistress of Louis XV, the Comtesse Du Barry (1743-93) was rejected in favour of the newly fashionable neo-Classical style, the distrust of erotic images and motifs was sealed.

Nevertheless, although it is important to remember that the Stoics and Epicureans retained their grip on many of those earnestly seeking happiness, the life of the senses and the passions was increasingly liberated and validated in the course of the century. They were encouraged to manifest themselves in different ways. 'Sensibilité' and 'Libertinage' are the terms which designate two of these ways.

2. *Sensibilité*

Far from denoting the self-interested heedlessness which the encouragement of sensual pleasures in a terrestrial paradise might be thought to incur, *sensibilité* emphasises the fundamental goodness of feelings that otherwise lie dormant. *Sensibilité* is a complex movement with many facets. This term designates a susceptibility to feelings, a capacity for emotion. A man might be sensitive to the charms of the gentle sex, and is allowed to be as sensitive as women to one's inner feelings, while both men and women are attuned, thanks to sensibility, to the harmony and beauty of nature. Strictly speaking, sensibility is not so much a form of happiness as a superior and desirable sort of unhappiness. Sensibility carries a notion of moral worth. Beaumarchais writes in the preface to his drama *La Mère coupable*. 'On est meilleur quand on se sent pleurer'. (You are a better person when you feel yourself crying). These sublime inner feelings could be made manifest by swooning or weeping. Many eighteenth-century writers do not, as one might expect, see in this feeble display of emotion the enemy of reason, but see it as tempering and refining our affinity with the natural and artistic world. Prévost's Des Grieux assures us that 'l'amour me rendait eclairé' (love enlightened me). His sensibility opens his heart but in a way that benefits his head. Sensibility carries a notion of class too. It has been argued that as real landscapes became more artificial and land was increasingly cultivated, gardens conversely became more natural and nature became associated with property. A sensitivity to natural feelings was therefore the product of a particular cultural disposition. Des Grieux declares that 'le commun des hommes n'est sensible qu'à cinq ou six passions [...] mais les personnes d'un caractère plus noble peuvent être remuées de mille façons différentes' (the common man is sensitive only to five or six passions [...] but people of a more noble character can be moved in a thousand different ways). His initially careful enumeration (cinq ou six passions) makes us more likely to accept the rampantly hyperbolic 'mille façons différentes' as real. Sensibility then not only opens hearts but doors. It means he can be trusted as a fundamentally good individual and exempts him from the accusations of evil that his actions and their effects seem to warrant. Although he murders, cheats at cards and lies to everyone, his sensibility represents an essence of goodness and may therefore excuse his waywardness. The manipulation of this spontaneity through the form of discourse is a mainstay of Prévost's novel. The contrivance of this spontaneity is highly effective in Des Grieux's hands. On one of many occasions when he is in a spot of bother he confides: 'Je me mis à verser un ruisseau de larmes avec toutes les marques du désespoir' (I took to pouring out a stream of tears with all the marks of desperation). That Des Grieux pulls out all the stops in a deliberate ploy to win sympathy is denoted by the slightly suspect reflexive verb 'se mettre' and the careful but seemingly superfluous addition of 'toutes les marques' on top of the fulsome metaphor. Sensibility is important not only on account of the truths which it unlocks but the abuses to which it is subject.

3. *Libertinage*

When the quest for happiness is supplanted by the pursuit of pleasure, we find ourselves in the domain of *libertinage*, a term that has no symmetrical counterpart in English. It tends to be translated as 'free thought', and indeed, unlike the joys depicted by Rococo painting, *libertinage* implies an intellectual freedom that accompanies and often authorises sexual liberties. But whereas sixteenth- and seventeenth-century *libertins* tended to be intellectuals committed to scepticism in one way or another, increasingly they are individuals, like Giacomo Casanova (1725-98), who wrote his infamous memoirs in French, given to sensual self-indulgence. *Libertinage* has no place for love. The Marquise de Merteuil, the *libertine* par excellence, outlines such an explicit code in letter 81 of the *Liaisons dangereuses*: 'je m'assurai que l'amour que l'on nous vante comme la cause de nos plaisirs, n'en est au plus que le prétexte' (I assured myself that the love vaunted as the cause of our pleasures is at best only a pretext for them). The same sort of sentiment, or lack of it, is expressed by the *libertin* Count in *Le Mariage de Figaro*: 'L'amour n'est que le roman du coeur, c'est le plaisir qui en est l'histoire' (Love is but the novel of the heart, pleasure is the history of it). History, characterised as solemn and faithful in comparison to the novel, is perhaps a surprising metaphor to come to the defence of pleasure which might not be supposed as true or serious as love. These beautifully textured aphorisms are truly *libertin*. They take a corresponding pleasure in the shapely forms that recommend it. Intellectual exhibitionism is in these cases as important as sensual fulfilment to *libertinage*.

In the eighteenth century *sensibilité* is in many ways a progenitor of *libertinage* which uses the same idioms. Nicolas-Edme Restif [or Rétif] de la Bretonne (1734-1806), a late eighteenth-century writer of *libertin* novels was influenced by the *sensibilité* of Rousseau's characters whom he transported into new and sometimes sordid urban scenes that earned him the title of 'le Rousseau du ruisseau' (the Rousseau of the gutter). However, it is to the Marquis de Sade (1740-1814) that we might turn to find the ultimate expression of libertinage. His *La Philosophie dans le boudoir* (1795), a series of dialogues urging the freedom of the passions, is dedicated 'aux libertins'. The preface begins thus:

Voluptueux de tous les âges et de tous les sexes, c'est à vous seuls que j'offre cet ouvrage: nourrissez-vous de ses principes, ils favorisent vos passions, et ces passions, dont de froids et plats moralistes vous effraient, ne sont que les moyens que la nature emploie pour faire parvenir l'homme aux vues qu'elle a sur lui; [...] ce n'est qu'en sacrifiant tout à la volupté, que le malheureux individu connu sous le nom d'homme, et jeté malgré lui sur ce triste univers, peut réussir à semer quelques roses sur les épines de la vie.

(Voluptuous people of all ages and all sexes, it is to you alone that I offer this work: feed on its principles, they will favour your passions, and these passions, from which cold and dull moralists frighten you, are only the means which nature employs to get man to reach the design which it has on him; [...] it is only by sacrificing all to sensuality that the unfortunate individual known by the name of man who is thrown in spite of himself into this sad universe can succeed in strewing some roses onto the thorns of life.)

The indulgence of one's passions is authorised by principles which rest on nature's laws. Sade has in common with many writers a desire to put man in touch with nature. But the *libertin* view here that sensation alone furnishes the possiblities of happiness draws pessimistically on an image of man abandoned in a hostile world. The final image of roses seems indebted more to the images favoured by *sensibilité* and the Rococo, but the 'semer' (sowing or strewing) possibly points to the prodigality which is synonymous with *libertinage* in the eighteenth century.

*

The Enlightenment recognised man's universal desire for and right to happiness, aiming through its pedagogical efforts to promote and secure this boon. 'Le bon bramin' (the good Brahmin), a philosophical chap positively bursting with knowledge and virtue in the very short Voltaire *conte, L'Histoire d'un bon Bramin* (1759), cannot seem to find the happiness that is supposed to result from knowledge and virtue. And he comes to the disturbing conclusion that it is precisely because he is endowed with these that he is denied happiness: 'plus il avait de lumières dans son entendement et de sensibilité dans son coeur, plus il était malheureux' (the more enlightened his understanding and the more sensitive his heart, the unhappier he was). Mystified by his own perversity, Voltaire's Brahmin realises that enlightenment is not conducive but, in many ways, actually preferable to happiness: 'si nous faisons cas du bonheur, nous faisons encore plus de cas de la raison' (if we set great store by happiness, we set even greater store by reason).

The Count's observation in the first scene of Beaumarchais's play, *Le Barbier de Séville* (1775) that 'chacun court après le bonheur' (everyone runs after happiness) makes happiness the object of a stampede rather than the fruit of serene intelligence. Perhaps looking at the marriage of the Count Almaviva and Rosine he has helped to broker, Figaro glimpses the melancholy truth that, like many others, they are happier seeking happiness than acquiring it. Once their ideal becomes a reality, it ceases to be ideal. The most poignant realisation of this kind is, however, reserved for Rousseau's *Julie, ou la nouvelle Héloïse* (1761) where, having settled into a life of virtue and satisfaction, Julie remarks that 'le bonheur m'ennuie' (happiness bores me). This candid observation reduces to tatters the eighteenth-century bid to reconcile virtue, knowledge and happiness.

However, if happiness had lost some of its sheen, so unhappiness could be redeemed as a virtue in itself. Just as eighteenth-century writers throw out the despotism of genius, so they overcome the despotism of perfection. Even in representing the real disasters and injustices to which we fall victim (as does *Candide* for example) or gloomily expatiating about the limitations of modern man (as does Rousseau), eighteenth-century writers articulate a positive view since optimism is a sign of passivity and contentment means indolence, while unhappiness is summoned by impatience with a reality that is ever susceptible of improvement.

Selected Reading

Christopher Berry, *The Idea of Luxury: A Conceptual and Historical Investigation* (Cambridge: Cambridge University Press, 1994). A book which shows how two thousand years of anti-luxury thought were turned on their head between 1690 and 1740.

Peter Brooks, *The Novel of Worldliness: Crébillon, Marivaux, Laclos, Stendhal* (Princeton: Princeton University Press, 1969). A work which covers the important *mondain* and *libertin* novels.

Norman Bryson, *Word and Image: French Painting of the Ancien Régime* (Cambridge: Cambridge University Press, 1981). Sophisticated study of the relations of paintings to texts in the period.

Albert O. Hirschman, *The Passions and the Interests: Political Arguments for Capitalism before Its Triumph* (Princeton: Princeton University Press, 1997). A study of the way passions became known and rehabilitated as 'interests' in the eighteenth century.

Janet Todd, *Sensibility: An Introduction* (London; New York: Methuen, 1986). Although interested chiefly in its English exponents, a very useful and interesting survey of the phenomenon of sensibility and all its ambivalence.

III
Philosophical Writings

Whether it was considered a passport to greater happiness, or merely a ticket to sorrowful uncertainty, philosophy remained central to the projects of the eighteenth century. Writers and thinkers agreed that, at least in recent history, their century was incomparably, supremely philosophical. But the thinkers of this proudly philosophical century were concerned first and foremost to understand what philosophy itself could be and who exactly philosophers, they themselves, might or should be. It will be apparent that their own conception of the philosopher differed from that of previous centuries and from that of our own, and that the works of the philosopher could take form in a number of different genres.

1. The 'Philosophe'

In Jean-Siméon Baptiste Chardin's painting, *Le Philosophe occupé de sa lecture* (the philosopher occupied by his reading), reading visibly induces a reverie. Chardin brilliantly suggests through the distant but intense gaze of his thinker the drift from rational understanding to a more speculative disposition. Here philosophical thought borders on the dream. Rousseau who admits that 'souvent mes méditations finissent par rêverie' (often my meditations finish in reverie) is not the only thinker in the Enlightenment to acknowledge the attraction of dreaming. In this painting, as elsewhere in the century, philosophy is not simply equated with the exercise of his reason. The Enlightenment did not (as certain nineteenth-century Romantics decided) consider the adversary of reason to be emotion but unreason. Accordingly, philosophical truths were not only delivered by reason, but could be yielded by dreams and speculation or even fictions and fantasies.

Chardin's painting of the philosopher reading was at first known as the chemist, or the alchemist. The gap between abstraction, speculation and experimental science had not opened yet, and the philosopher was entitled to dabble in the diverse areas which knowledge was colonising. Above all, the philosopher was widely supposed to be motivated by specific polemical views and committed to a particular political stance. In the eighteenth century the term 'philosophe' does not neutrally designate a capacity for apprehending or exploring truth, but, pejoratively or sympathetically, it denotes an individual of a particular persuasion, such that we talk of the *philosophes* rather than philosophers in the eighteenth century. Charles Palissot de Montenoy's play, *Les Philosophes* (1760), is levelled satirically at a number of controversial contemporary figures, such as Diderot and Rousseau, and no-one will have expected it to discuss any philosophers from other ages.

The eighteenth-century *philosophes* were not to be exalted as bygone thinkers 'voyaging through seas of thought alone' (as Wordsworth imagined Newton) had been. They were part of a community and their philosophy should be subservient to it. Many philosophers in eighteenth-century France see themselves primarily as writers. Ideally, they were not to know they were philosophers. Voltaire makes clear that not all people are susceptible to philosophical wisdom, but in the same breath as he restricts the constituency of philosophy he broadens the definition of the philosopher. As he puts it in the preface to his *Dictionnaire philosphique portatif*, published in 1764:

> En un mot les ouvrages de la philosophie ne sont faits que pour les philosophes, et tout honnête homme doit chercher à être philosophe, sans se piquer de l'être.

> (In a word works of philosophy are only written for philosophers and every civilised being must seek to be a philosopher without priding himself on it.)

Apparently contradictory definitions, at once exclusive and inclusive, cluster around the philosopher. The philosopher is the eighteenth-century counterpart to the *honnête homme*, the fundamentally decent, moderate individual cherished by many writers of the seventeenth century. Indeed, Voltaire's statement recalls the syntax of La Rochefoucauld's definition that 'le vrai honnête homme est celui qui ne se pique de rien' (the true *honnête homme* is the person who does not become angry about anything). The *Encyclopédie*'s definition of the *philosophe* as 'un honnête homme qui veut plaire et se rendre utile' (a civilised being who wishes to please and make himself useful) makes this lineage clear.

It is the decency and common sense evinced by a father negoti-ating the difficulties of a particular domestic crisis that entitle Vanderk to be considered a philosopher in *Le Philosophe sans le savoir* (1765), a play which Michel-Jean Sedaine wrote in order to counter the claims of Palissot's play and to advertise the qualities of the philosopher. Some critics were, however, vexed that such a man should be called a philosopher. Vanderk is a philosopher inas-much that philosophy now consists of behaving reasonably, even if that means instinctively. He is worthy of Voltaire's definition pre-cisely in failing to know that he is a philosopher, for a true philosopher need not know, let alone write, anything in particular. Marivaux's eponymous *l'Indigent Philosophe, ou l'homme sans souci* (1727), and the inhabitant of the *Cabinet du philosophe* (1734, also by Marivaux) are creatures of the same species, who delight simply in casting a discerning eye over their society. The 'indigent philosophe' breaks off to eat and explains that he will resume his work when it is light. Such desultory words on society are inter-rupted and circumscribed, as Diderot's dialogues later will be, by the rhythms and realities of everyday existence.

This modest disposition becomes a chief prerequisite for the new type of philosopher. *Le Philosophe ignorant* (1766), the unpromising title given to a series of philosophical remarks written by Voltaire, can be considered an entirely serious and appropriate figure to be entrusted with the task of philosophical exposition. Rousseau likewise rejects the notion of thought as an exalted form of activity. In the preface to *Narcisse*, his play first performed in 1752, he militates against the idea that philosophy consists of pro-found intellectual reflection by explaining that: 'L'homme fut né pour penser et non pour réfléchir' (man was born to think and not to reflect). The difference between thought and reflection is that, as Narcissus will tell us, reflection is dangerous. It is self-regarding rather than a spontaneous, healthy natural activity. This nuance corresponds to Rousseau's subsequent distinction between a healthy nourishing 'amour de soi' or self-love and the pernicious 'amour-propre' or pride which feeds on the gaze of others. Like the other thinkers, Rousseau attempts to equate proper philosophy or thought with a healthy, natural activity devoid of prestige. It is as if philosophers are experimentally emptied of as many attributes as possible to see at what points they seem and cease to be philosophical. All these writers conclude that philosophy should ideally amount to a more humble quotidian wisdom. Learning is to be worn as lightly and loosely as their old dressing gowns.

This modest disposition entails a new respect for the reader as an equal and accounts for the forms that many eighteenth-century philosophical explorations take. Writers and readers are no longer divided by a great distance across which the philosopher must shout didactically, but they become confidents and friends. Voltaire envisages an encounter between reader and writer where both commit an equal amount of effort into constructing the text. He maintains that the reader should do half of the work. 'C'est au lecteur de faire la moitié' (it is up to the reader to do half). Like many of his characters we are to inhabit a halfwayhouse between the passive acceptance and total distrust of the author's opinions. This corresponds to the thrust of Voltaire's thought in general, with its resolute rejection of absolutism but its equally firm belief in authority, be it a distant deistic God or its ideal political counterpart, a constitutional monarch. Much philosophy is written in the first person and does not disguise but exhibit its roots in the consciousness of a particular individual who confides without confidence. Voltaire's philosophical tales are largely the medium by which he tries to achieve this relationship, while Diderot uses dialogues to the same end.

2. Philosophical Fictions

Eighteenth-century writers do not tend to use the word 'fiction' with the stark contrast to 'fact' that is now implicit, but they regard truth as amenable to different methods. It is thought that fiction, whether the ideas contrived by intuition, speculation or the invention of novelists, can entertain insights to which pure reason cannot always accede. Fictions appeal for different reasons to the philosophically inclined writers and readers of the Enlightenment. A solace from the pangs of absolutism, they are an expedient for masking truths that would otherwise be too dangerous to venture. But they can also deliberately and enthusiastically render difficult the task of delineating fiction and reality. Fictional narratives expose some of the artficial ways we impose onto the discrete events of life a structure that confers sense. As those who have read Diderot's *Jacques le fataliste* (begun c.1771) will know particularly, philosophical novels do not always proceed by making philosophy easy, but they sometimes prefer to make reading difficult.

The great eighteenth-century passion for tales and fables might, however, seem at odds with its predilection for enlightenment, even if it considers fictions to be acceptable. Childish fables were denied to children by the tutor in Rousseau's treatise on education, *Emile* (1762), but in part because he considered them to be consonant with the ambitions and values of the Enlightenment. The *Histoires, ou contes de temps passé* (1691-1695) by Charles Perrault (1628-1703) had remained extremely popular in the eighteenth century and were rivalled only by Antoine Galland's version of the *Arabian nights*, published under the title of *Les Mille et une nuits* between 1704 and 1716. This fairytale with its dreamy and erotic scenes perhaps recommends itself also to the writers and readers of the Enlightenment because it is the story of the power of the story. Through her tales, Scheherazade defers her death sentence and resists power wielded cruelly and despotically. The life-saving powers of her tales affirm the restlessly, endlessly, inventive spirit of man in the shadow of injustice.

All these elements, as well as many others, are compressed into one of the most famous works of the century, the philosophical tale, *Candide, ou de l'optimisme*, first published in 1759, expurgated for centuries since and still to be found on the papal index of banned books.

Voltaire, Candide *(1759)*

The *conte philosophique* (philosophical tale) is a highly adaptable form minted by Voltaire. Like the good philosopher, the *conte philosophique* does not take pride in the position it adopts. It chooses rather to hide its philosophical badges under a fictional cloak. *Zadig* (1748) purports to be a whimsy, apparently the result of 'le plaisir de n'avoir rien à faire' (the pleasure of having nothing to do), yet, tantalisingly, the *conte* also promises 'plus qu'il ne semble dire' (more than it seems to say). The *contes* seem playfully inconsequential yet are replete with allusions to historical and philosophical controversies of the day.

In the preface to *Candide*, Voltaire playfully exploits the eighteenth-century convention by which authors try to pass off their fictions as texts which they have merely edited or translated, writings found elsewhere, out in the real world. Inauspiciously, this text on optimism was apparently found in the pockets of a Dr. Ralph at Minden (where the Seven Years War, 1756-63, happened to be raging) who is, unfortunately, dead. This is the first of many rejoinders to the optimism that is the text's subject. *Candide* has a devastating effect in part because what seems to be fictional turns out to be disconcertingly real. It moves between pure fantasy and recent history, suggesting that events like the execution of Admiral Byng (in a court-martial in 1757) or the auto-da-fé (a religiously motivated execution) which Candide gets to see, should be fictional. Voltaire's cocktail of fiction and history devastatingly impresses upon us how miserable human life is, as it moves from one truly horrific disaster to the next. Written only four years after the Lisbon earthquake in 1755 and during the Seven Years War, *Candide* reflects Voltaire's preoccupations wih cruelty and injustice in that period. It is the riposte to the argument of Leibniz (1646-1716) who argued that even if evil existed in the world, as it manifestly did, it was a minimal amount of evil that might be contributing to a greater good, and that this was therefore the best of all possible worlds. Pangloss, Leibniz's pupil and Candide's teacher, never forsakes this belief in 'le meilleur des mondes possible' even in the face of all the atrocities that Voltaire throws his way. Pangloss's beliefs rest on the simple and indubitable truth that he is a philosopher, even if he cannot think or argue like one, and these are the opinions a philosopher ought to have. Unlike the ideal *philosophes* who pursue their interests, indifferent to their status, Pangloss, we might say, 'se pique de l'être' (takes pride in being it).

Voltaire's tale allows him to launch devastating attacks both on the philosophical schools which tolerate and pretend to understand evil and suffering and on the institutions (like the church or the crown) which, in many cases, cause this suffering.

Voltaire had written *contes* before in which the vagaries of fortune and its apparent indifference to man had disturbed. But in *Zadig*, for instance, the essentially good character and intelligence of the archetypal man of reason, Zadig, can cope with all the adversity he meets. These chance events which assault his character also affirm it. They are character building. Critics have agreed that, conversely, Candide has no character, but, as Roger Pearson has put it, he is a blank page on which experience writes itself. As a result, *Zadig* could be compared to a jigsaw in which we have to admit that some pieces are missing, although enough are left to make sense of the full picture. In *Candide*, however, not only have more pieces gone missing, but the picture that we are trying to construct has been lost or, more depressingly, has never been known.

Candide moves us from one episode to the next at a great tempo with no explanations or justifications. No conjunctions can meaningfully link the consecutive and episodic events through which the narrative races. Extravagantly short chapters are made to look even smaller by their long titles. In a hideously complicated world we are left only with a series of simple pasts. Pangloss's beliefs are more fictional than Voltaire's fiction which refuses to move in a predictable and plausible way from a beginning to a happy end. We are never allowed to believe and bask in the illusion of a coherent fiction. The illusion is invaded from one flank by the violent forces of history (with Voltaire's references to terrible events of recent history) and, on the other, by a riotous mass of artifices (as Voltaire brings back characters from the dead and multiplies and mocks the conventions of stories). *Candide* teases us into being Pangloss, into trying to construct sense. This is indeed what we want and expect of a good story, but *Candide* repeatedly offers conclusions only to retract them from us before the final ambiguous ending.

Candide, like some of the other *contes*, resists a holistic view of the world. Parts are lumped together in an unwholesome way. The whole is not greater than the sum of its parts, but is merely a pile of them. Human bodies are not an inherent purposeful whole. Whereas Candide is taught that eyes are made to see, legs to walk and noses to carry spectacles, he learns that bodies are subject to torture or amputation. The old woman without a buttock, the slave without a left hand and a right leg and Pangloss without one eye are not granted the relief of death, but are reminded of the amorphous and meaningless shape of existence. Voltaire shares the century's interest in the instructive properties of impotence. Once denied sight, the characters in Voltaire's *contes* (Memnon and 'le crocheteur borgne', the one-eyed locksmith), tend to gain insight. Equally, by accepting that we have a partial (in other words both partisan and restricted) view of the world, we can resist the folly of totalising views and systems. This blurred vision is the only tenable response to a world without meaning. 'Le secret d'ennuyer est de tout dire' (the secret of boring people is to spell out everything). But it is not only more boring, but dangerous to hide a partial view under a stance which purports to understand absolutely and to say all which is, after all, the prerogative of Pangloss (all talk).

Nevertheless, for all the horrors it stages and the uncertainties it generates, *Candide* knows how to delight us, and we will want to reread it. This is partly because the disasters are mitigated by the ironic intelligence that lies behind and shares them with us. *Candide* is full of the woeful stories of its characters, sometimes trying to upstage one another in their suffering. But in both telling and hearing stories, the evil that is their subject seems to be neutralised, and we feel once again that we are human in an inhuman world: 'Ils disputèrent quinze jours de suite, et au bout de quinze jours ils étaient aussi avancés que le premier. Mais enfin ils parlaient, ils se communiquaient des idées, ils se consolaient.' (They argued for fifteen days in a row and after fifteen days they got no further on the fifteenth day than they had on the first. But ultimately they were talking, exchanging ideas and consoling one another). Like the *Mille et une nuits, Candide* tests and proves the capacity of both characters and reader to withstand the assaults of the world through stories.

Stories are valuable not because they can impart truths but because, however inhuman their subjects, they restore us as humans. It is in such interactions that Voltaire sees humans in all their glory. But it is a glory which shines on our limitations. The good Brahmin in the *conte* of that name knows that he cannot answer any fundamental questions and that his disquisitions lead nowhere: He admits, 'je parle beaucoup, et je demeure confus et honteux de moi-même après avoir parlé' (I speak a lot, and I remain confused and ashamed of myself after having spoken). But the *conte* is no better and ends by suggesting that, short of coming to any conclusions, it itself can only invite further discussion. Its simple final sentence encourages rather than shames people like the Brahmin: 'Il y a là de quoi parler beaucoup' (that leaves us with a lot to talk about).

Like the stories that contribute to them, our best conversations are a stimulus to further conversations rather than the route to any conclusions. If, God forbid, we did know the Truth, there would be less to talk about. Uncertainty is the motor of conversation, but eighteenth-century philosophers do see other virtues than the wisdom of uncertainty in the many dialogues they conduct and write.

3. Conversation and Dialogue

Like the 'bon Bramin', the philosophers of the eighteenth century talked a lot. They talked perhaps more than the philosophers of any age before and since, and their writing is full of talking. Conversation was an art refined and sharpened in the *salon*, the term that designates the social space where, presided over by a particular woman whose presence vouchsafes the grace and the intelligibility of all that is said, philosophers, writers and wits would meet to exchange ideas. At least until its last years, the century overwhelmingly favours the *salon* as the context for its intellectual enterprises. Here knowledge is spoken and ideas discussed. The importance of speaking, and speaking well rather than rigorously, is paramount.

Many writers hear their words spoken rather than seeing them read. Like Marivaux's 'indigent philosophe' they reckon with being quoted rather than analysed. The spoken word seems to commit us intuitively to common sense which is often betrayed when it takes expression in systematic or written form. When asked a difficult question, Voltaire's *bête noire*, Leibniz, flees the embarrassment of oral engagement and takes cover in the written word: 'Leibniz ne sut que répondre. Aussi fit-il de gros livres dans lesquels il ne s'entendait pas' (Leibniz did not know what to say in reply. Therefore he wrote big books in which he could not understand himself).

Dialogues have been used as a pedagogical tool ever since Plato's Socratic dialogues. Bernard le Bovier de Fontenelle's *Entretiens sur la pluralité des mondes* (1686), which popularised Descartes's ideas in conversations between a philosopher and a lady whose hesitant comprehension authorises our own understanding of the ideas, remained influential above all in suggesting that the process of learning could be accompanied by pleasure. While d'Alembert remarks in the *Discours préliminaire* that philosophical discussions are reducing the levity of society conversation, others maintain that, far from diluting the pleasures of society, the encounter of philosophy and conversation renders these discussions and their subjects sexy. Moi, in the *Neveu de Rameau*, embodies his thoughts in this way: 'mes pensées, ce sont mes catins' (my thoughts are my prostitutes). Diderot is one of many eighteenth-century writers who specialises in dialogue, but he it is perhaps who takes the form to its limits. *Le Rêve de d'Alembert* both exemplifies his use of the dialogue to advance complex ideas and a tendency for the dialogue to pour forth ideas that it cannot contain.

Diderot, Le Rêve de d'Alembert *(1769)*

Denis Diderot (1713-84) is the chief exponent of the dialogue which entertains speculative ideas about philosophical questions. With a series of self-generating conversations and stories, like those spun by Voltaire's *contes*, Diderot's novel *Jacques le fataliste* (begun 1771 and posthumously published) pursues complex ideas concerning freewill and its limitations. A belief in the impotence of freewill in the face of a world where one event was simply caused by a previous one in an endless chain was known as determinism. Diderot, in common with many other eighteenth-century philosophers, also speculated about materialism, the idea that all was matter in the world and that the thoughts and feelings of people were determined by their particular physical constitution. In his dialogue, *Le Rêve de d'Alembert*, Diderot assembles several figures (all contemporaries of his: the eminent doctor Théophile Bordeu, Mlle de Lespinasse and d'Alembert) in order to discuss such ideas. They conclude in a speculative way that even our mental and spiritual operations can be attributed to physical and biological factors and that in a constantly changing world without a God, inanimate matter can evolve into animate forms.

Le Rêve de d'Alembert combines the latest scientific research with conversational and anecdotal moments to produce a work that speculates, informs and entertains as so many of Diderot's dialogues do. It resembles other philosophical dialogues in allowing one of the voices of the dialogue to prevail in a helpful pedagogical way. Bordeu explains his radical ideas about the formation of matter through a series of metaphors which carry philosophy into the realms of ordinary life. The nature of the changing world is for instance encapsulated by the image of a beehive, the human brain envisaged as a spider in its web, the character of man conceptualised as a clavichord that plays itself. These metaphors not only aid our comprehension of the particular questions they illuminate, but in sum they correspond to a world where mind and matter can become one another, where oppositions between the realm of pure thought and daily life ought to be broken down. With these metaphors Diderot emphasises that, complex as it is, philosophy consists not in the acquisition of learning, but in a sensitivity to the phenomena of everyday life. The untutored interlocutor of the scientists and philosophers, Mlle de Lespinasse, realises that she not only understands, but always has implicitly engaged with, the philosophical subject under discussion. Like the *philosophe ignorant* or *le philosophe sans le savoir*, she is a philosopher who takes no pride in her position. She now realises: 'J'ai fait de la philosophie sans m'en douter' (I have been philosophising without knowing it).

She is borrowing Monsieur Jourdain's line from Molière's *Le bourgeois gentilhomme,* 'j'ai fait de la prose sans que je m'en aperçusse' (I've been speaking prose without noticing it). She is an *arriviste* in the world of philosophy – only not as the butt of comedy. Philosophy brings down the barriers of class and gender, for this *philosophe* is not an *honnête homme* but an *honnête femme.*

Diderot favours the dialogue form in that it gives the impression that it could have happened or did once happen. The words belong to particular individuals. It must have happened at a particular time in a particular place. When they converse the implication is that on another day at another time in this changing world the dialogue might well have taken a different form. Accordingly, the dialogue is not always fluent and coherent. It is interrupted here by the sleep of d'Alembert, while in the *Lettre sur les aveugles* the exchange is curtailed by the death of the blind man. These provisional or terminal interruptions appear to disturb the coherence and assurance of the ideas ventured and remind us of the patterns of life that remain indifferent to our discussions. However, precisely because they are asleep or dying and lapse into monologues, these figures seem to gain a privileged access to truths which cannot be unlocked by reason nor voiced by civil dialogue. This tactlessness lends their ideas an authority and aura. D'Alembert's dream is such a moment where, with intuitive brilliance, he expounds radical ideas about the origin of the world. In Diderot's dramas and in his dialogue, *Le Neveu de Rameau* dialogue is likewise pushed aside by the silencing force of an overwhelming emotion or an immediate truth.

The dialogue sympathises and engages with a world which is made up of different parts that cannot be synthesised. Sometimes Diderot includes himself, or at least his name, in the dialogue of which he is the author. This entry into the text corresponds to the sense that there exists no clear division between creating and created forces, and we are reminded of the difficulties which ensue when we try to understand a phenomenon of which we are part. The dialogue acts as a stimulus for ideas that need to jump from one consciousness to another and are developed by this traffic. If Voltaire declares that 'j'écris pour agir' (I write in order to act) we may suppose that Diderot might have said 'j'écris pour penser' (I write in order to think). Diderot collaborates with other thinkers in many projects, whether in reacting to or working with them. They are never far away. As Flaubert puts it quite simply in his comical dictionary of clichéd definitions, the *Dictionnaire des idées reçues*: 'Diderot: suivi de d'Alembert' (Diderot: followed by d'Alembert). He thus anticipates the modern notion of scientific research as a product of teamwork rather than the province of genius. Dialogues, however, not only encourage collaboration but reveal fragmentation, and later dialogues, such as *Le Neveu de Rameau* or Rousseau's *Dialogues*, give expression to internal divisions, as the individual is stalked and teased by the shadow it itself projects.

*

The nonchalance essential to the *philosophes* and visible in their witty fictions and elegant dialogues should not mask their anger and their urgency. Insouciance and effortlessness were ostensibly prized by French eighteenth-century culture, but it is typical that behind the elegant façades of 'Sans souci' ('Without a care', as Frederick the Great called his palace in Potsdam) paced one of the most anxious, restless and belligerent of monarchs. If philosophers were to be homely and modest figures it was so that their philosophy might be useful and natural, harnessed to virtue and happiness, as the *Encyclopédie* makes clear. They were to lead campaigns for reform and clamour for change.

In the eighteenth century, philosophy is widely construed to be a pursuit whose value is sanctioned by the benefits derived by the wider population to which it appeals. Ideally, the philosopher is a good man, his philosophy useful. Philosophy is then above all perceived to be a useful device which can go towards making life more enjoyable. The *Encyclopédie* is not ashamed to place questions of husbandry and the weaving of Turkish carpets alongside disquisitions on philosophical matters, for, however modestly and locally, they too contribute to the happiness of mankind. The conviction that knowledge largely or only has value if it is useful accounts for the Enlightenment's methods in many quarters. But such convictions also explain many of the doubts and reservations about the Enlightenment to which this age also gives expression.

Selected Reading

Geoffrey Bremner, *Order and Chance* (Cambridge: Cambridge University Press, 1983). A study of Diderot's works and ideas.

Thomas M. Kavanagh, *Enlightenment and The Shadows of Chance: The Novel and the Culture of Gambling in Eighteenth-Century France* (London; Baltimore: Johns Hopkins University Press, 1993). A persuasive account of the role of chance in Enlightenment literature.

Friedrich Albert Lange, *The History of Materialism* (London: Routledge and Kegan Paul, 1950). Contains useful chapters on materialist philosophy in the eighteenth century.

Roger Pearson, *The Fables of Reason: A Study of Voltaire's* Contes philosophiques (Oxford: Oxford University Press, 1993). An entertaining and stimulating study of the *conte*.

Jack Undank and Herbert Josephs, eds, *Diderot, Digression and Dispersion: A Bicentennial Tribute*, (French Forum Publishers, Lexington, Kentucky, 1984). A collection of essays by the Diderot experts on his form over the full range of his texts.

IV

Doubts about Philosophy

The philosopher has been idealised as a figure who does not philosophise self-consciously, yet this figure increasingly encourages forms of self-interest and self-assertion which had hitherto been scorned. Some writers are anxious that the philosophical advances of the Enlightenment are designed to gratify self-interest rather than support virtue. Others, including those promoting new forms of philosophy and observing its new potential, question the directions that it is taking. While Voltaire has no illusions that rational thought will remain the preserve of an elite fit for absorbing it and is convinced that the greater part of the population would remain indifferent to the ideas of the Enlightenment, others regret that philosophy in the eighteenth century is courting too large a public. In his *Essai sur la société des gens de lettres et les grands* (1753), d'Alembert observes that in committing oneself to making philosophy useful to a wider public, it loses its inherent value and risks becoming hostage to the whim of others. Value is then determined by the capricious view of others rather than the force of its internal logic. He goes on to argue that the only intellectual activity with which one would persist on a desert island was geometry since its value is not determined by others. The same view is voiced more insistently by Jean-Jacques Rousseau who, retreating imaginatively and at last actually to an island of his own where he can experience primary, original truths in isolation, marks the most radical departure from the philosophical assumptions that underpin the Enlightenment. The confidence of the Enlightenment would be shaken once and for all, at least among those who cared to listen to Jean-Jacques.

1. Rousseau's *Discours* (1750 & 1754)

Rousseau's career had begun conventionally enough. He headed from his native Geneva to Paris to become a man of letters. There he was moderately successful with a number of plays and operas. As a promising young writer destined to become a pleasantly mediocre one, it is possible to say that, like a certain politician, he already had a brilliant future behind him. It was on his way to see Diderot in Vincennes prison that he had, as he later claimed, his 'illumination' which would lead to the publication of the *Discours sur les sciences et les arts* (1750) that won the prize of the Academy of Dijon and changed the course of his life. Rousseau's support of the beleaguered man of letters (evinced by his visit of Diderot), a familiar cry sounded by such tireless campaigners as Voltaire, was to turn into a more radical and original sense of alienation which would result not only in antagonistic exile from society and its authorities but a more profound and agonised distance from his fellow writers and humans.

However, at the very beginning of this discourse Rousseau tricks us into validating a perspective which, it transpires, he does not share. This eloquent eulogy appears to approve with enthusiasm the achievements of the Enlightenment:

> C'est un grand et beau spectacle de voir l'homme sortir en quelque manière du néant par ses propres efforts, par les lumières de sa raison les ténèbres dans lesquelles la nature l'avait enveloppé; s'élever au-dessus de lui-même; s'élancer par l'esprit jusque dans les régions célestes; parcourir à pas de géant, ainsi que le soleil, la vaste étendue de l'univers; et, ce qui est encore plus grand et plus difficile, rentrer en soi pour y étudier l'homme et connaître sa nature, ses devoirs et sa fin. Toutes ces merveilles se sont renouvelées depuis peu de générations.

> (It is a great and beautiful sight to see man emerging from as it were nothing through his own efforts, emerging through the enlightenment of his reason from the darkness in which nature had enveloped him; rising up above himself; thrusting forward with his intelligence into the celestial regions; traversing with giant steps the

vast expanse of the universe, just like the sun; and, what is even
greater and more difficult, returning into himself to study man
there and to know his nature, his duties and his purpose. All these
miracles have been repeated only in recent generations.)

It is a beautiful passge, but suspiciously so. With its hyperbole,
its grandiose image of giant steps (in a vocabulary which prefigures
that of Neil Armstrong), its progression from 'ténèbres' to 'soleil',
its shifting focus from exploration to introspection, we might
imagine the sight described to be the quintessential mission statement of the Enlightenment. Indeed it would serve as a good
summary of its ambitions and satisfaction in achieving them. All
these 'merveilles' seem to be accredited here. But Rousseau, like
all the *philosophes*, does not believe in miracles. For a start, the
'grand et beau spectacle' looks impressive in a rather superficial
way and is immediately qualified in view of the greater difficulty of
'rentrer en soi'. Rousseau indeed recoils from this superficial sight
in order to elaborate a vision of his own. He then goes on to show
how this self-satisfaction is misplaced. Rousseau argues that the arts
and sciences are the garlands on our chains. Rather than allowing
us to think freely and differently, the arts and the sciences perpetuate the divisions in society with their coteries and conventions
and merely reflect the prejudices of the day.

This passage proves that one has to work within the existing discourses in order to challenge them. For Voltaire and others,
Rousseau's tendency to write against writing is a contradiction that
is confounding. But Rousseau makes the point that it was and is
possible for him to play this game. These stances are not contradictory. Rather these experiences prove Jean-Jacques's point.
Firstly, the texture of this passage allows Rousseau to show that his
stance cannot be explained as sour grapes but that he has been a
writer with all the attributes and gifts required of him. Secondly
and more importantly, he is showing that he could play this game
in which you need not say what you believe. The fact that he can
deceive in talking deceptively like this proves his point. When you
write you adopt other identities, adopt certain conventions and
bow to them. The first discourse, on the sciences and the arts, has
to precede the second which talks of man in general. Any discus-

sion of morality or philosophy must first take account of the text's complicity in the conventions which it seeks to expose.

The first discourse makes clear that we live in a climate of moral decadence. The examples of Sparta and Rome allow us to see what has gone wrong. The empirical, moral view of the turmoil in contemporary society was awarded a prize probably for being well-written and enjoyably contrary, but in a second discourse Rousseau launches into a more unpredictable essay to explain why this is the case. Rousseau now seeks the origin of this evil in his *Discours sur l'origine et les fondements de l'inégalité parmi les hommes*, known as the second discourse. This is a common procedure in the Enlightenment. The legitimacy of the contemporary political system is, for instance, the subject of a discussion between camps led respectively by Montesquieu and Henri de Boulainvilliers who explore the origins of the French state to find the principles they believe enshrined in the state. Rousseau, however, shocks once again. The search for these origins is ordinarily conducted by a mixture of theoretical argument and historical fact. Rousseau flies in the face of this sophisticated historiography with a peremptory cry, 'Écartons les faits' (let's dispense with facts). Descartes had objected to history as the science only of likelihoods, and even historians such as Voltaire were embarrassed by the Pyrrhonist or sceptical objections and strains. Descartes objected that history was an obstacle blocking the destination of purely rational knowledge. But Rousseau does not care about the veracity of facts. As the subtitle of his *Du Contrat social, Principes du droit politique* (principles of political right), indicates, Rousseau is more interested in rights.

Rousseau's method of seeking a state of nature which may not have existed constitutes a serious attack on the empirical, historically grounded method cherished by the Enlightenment. The first discourse questions its assumptions and ideals, the second its methods in pursuing them and the conclusions to which they lead. This fictional, hypothetical model foreshadows the use of fiction in Rousseau's case to produce truths of which history and philosophy are not capable. The preface to his bestselling novel *Julie, ou la nouvelle Héloïse* (1761) later makes clear that the vision elicited by the novel can usefully replace all the redundant insights of these rational disciplines. Speculation, as used by Rousseau in the second discourse, allows him to develop the undervalued imagination in understanding affectively and intuitively that for which history cannot account.

Rousseau tries to disengage from histories of facts a narrative of rights. Facts do not confer rights: Because, as a matter of fact, someone is bigger than you does not mean, as a matter of principle, that they should be. But theorists, says Rousseau, have deduced from a set of facts a series of rights. Hobbes was not wrong to say that some people were manifestly stronger than others in constructing his model of the monarchic state, but the so-called 'droit du plus fort' (the right of the strongest) is merely a fact. It is wrong to structure society on that basis, for if we look at a state of nature divested of the arbitrary social structures which have been imposed onto it, we realise that man is solitary with no thought of inequality. Natural inequality cannot justify social inequalities. In the state of nature inequality does not matter, but society freezes these differences and makes them matter. Rousseau accounts for man's development from this original state by explaining that society was a fluke, a 'concours fortuit de plusieurs causes étrangères qui ne pouvaient jamais naître' (a fortuitous concatenation of several extrinsic causes which could never have come about). It was not inevitable and intrinsic.

Beneath the sedimentation of human laws over the ages Rousseau then seeks a reservoir of immutable principles which can guide us to an understanding of the malaise that is identified in the first discourse. What Rousseau's method allows him to see, once the layers have been peeled off, is that society itself is inessential. Ideas of society, which is necessarily historical and contingent, have been imported into the state of nature. Rousseau, it has been observed, is then the first to see society itself as a problem. Other eighteenth-century writers were equally, perhaps more acutely, aware of injustices, but believed that their lines of philosophical enquiry would take them to solutions. If the existence of God could be determined on a more rational basis and fanaticism were eliminated, then undoubtedly society would be more agreeable. If man could understand the vagaries of the natural world or the nature of human consciousness, as Montesquieu or Hume tried, then likewise society would be improved. They therefore consider

social problems as subsets of larger, more demanding philosophical questions. As Hayden White puts it, 'Enlightenment thinkers
regarded the commendable aspects of their own societies as func-
tions of essentially harmonious natural processes while deplorable
aspects were residues of primitive misunderstandings of how
nature worked'. Rousseau is then an exception in viewing society
itself as a problem. Social existence is paradoxical and no amount
of intellectual progress or such philosophical enquiry could alle-
viate this. A social problem requires social means. Rousseau
proposes this transformation of society in his *Du contrat social* (his
treatise on political right published in 1762).

In the second discourse, Rousseau's emotional and imaginative
investment is greater than it was in the first discourse. His hypothetical speculation is bolder, as he consults nature through his
heart, a recess of sentiment and insight untainted by society. This
interplay of rational argument and emotional appeals is designed
to lend a coherence to the otherwise fragmented self. *Du contrat
social,* however, adopts a different style. Here he shows that he is
not seeking a transcendent solution but attempting to rethink
society within the limitations he has already noted. It is in many
ways the most innovative work of the age, but is also conservative.
Rousseau proposes this model of government for small nations
and argues that nations such as Russia cannot be transformed but
only changed from within if the characteristics and customs of its
people are inherently different. Unlike Voltaire and Montesquieu,
he is not attempting to divide power by multiplying the outlets it
can find or giving voice to plural or minority groups. Instead he
seeks a homogeneity where all citizens speak with same voice.
Hence readings of Rousseau which see him as the theorist of a
totalitarian society have been possible. There is certainly something disturbingly dry and restrictive about a work ostensibly
opening up access to the state. As Patrick Coleman has said, divergent responses to the text seem to shut you out just as you are
excluded from the Republic if you dissent. Coleman argues that
Rousseau's paradoxical style deliberately reminds us of the difficulties in evaluating political concepts and finding linguistic
processes that do not betray interests, urging the reader to 'adopt
a more critical, independent attitude' and provide the checks and

balances which are not foreseen by the theoretical scheme on the level of discourse itself.

Rousseau is perhaps at his most scrupulous here in attempting to resist the eloquence and brilliance which he sees as the facile hallmarks of superficial discourses but which he can command all too easily. In the two discourses, as elsewhere in his oeuvre, Rousseau makes clear his loathing of the specious power that the writers of the Enlightenment could deploy and its potential to exacerbate and generate further divisions. D'Alembert stated in the *Discours préliminaire* that ideas and passions could combine to form a pungent cocktail. We saw earlier that he hints at the potentially sinister power of eloquence in silencing even reason observing that 'les prodiges qu'elle opère souvent entre les mains d'un seul sur toute une nation sont peut-être le témoignage le plus éclatant de la supériorité d'un homme sur un autre' (the wonders that it performs in the hands of a single man over a whole nation bear perhaps the most spectacular testimony to the superiority of one man over another). This may be a tribute to the force of the great man but it does not hide somewhat sinister undertones about its seductive powers. 'Prodiges' and 'Éclatant' are not the indices of rational discourse but, like the 'merveilles' accredited by Rousseau, they are double-edged. The union of ideas and passions effected by eloquence is both exploited and dreaded by Rousseau. Voltaire, in trying to approximate the intensity of religious discourse, also attempts to borrow this despotic power, and Des Grieux in Prévost's *Manon Lescaut* admits (for honesty is itself rhetorically useful at times) to relying on his 'éloquence scolastique' (scholastic eloquence) to fetch him out of sticky situations.

It has been said that the progress of Enlightenment can be measured by tracing a path from the dictionary of doubts, Pierre Bayle's *Dictionnaire historique et critique* (published first in two volumes in 1697, then in four in 1704), to the *Encyclopedie*, the record of achievements. However, this impressive upward trajectory should not hide the energies devoted to explorations of the other directions. While Rousseau was scoffed at for being as hopelessly pastoral and nostalgic as early eighteenth-century figures had been perceived to be, and Palissot wittily depicted him on all fours, his idea that the arts and sciences are merely garlands on the chains which bind us reverberates in the later years of the century. Some thinkers realised that, far from looking back, Rousseau was looking ahead and trying to avert the continuing degradation and moral regression that the century was witnessing. His insight that we are bewitched by competition with one another and tainted by the duplicity which festers in society finds expression in *Les Liaisons dangereuses*, perhaps the most frightening and compelling demonstration of the fearful coincidence of passions and ideas.

2. Laclos, *Les Liaisons dangereuses* (1784)

Les Liaisons dangereuses, published to great acclaim in 1784, both brings together and questions, in an implicit way, many of the philosophical trends of the past years. It examines the moral consequences of beliefs in materialism and questions the possible value of enlightenment without exempting its own methods and purposes from such scrutiny. It is by no means clear whether the novel is extolling the intelligence of the central characters, Merteuil and Valmont, or deploring the consequences to which this intelligence leads. It is for the reader, presented with two mutually exclusive prefaces and a series of letters that can be read from different perspectives, to decide. But it is clear that the marriage of reason and virtue of which the Enlightenment dreamed has been annulled.

If Rousseau, who is quoted throughout the letters by Merteuil and Valmont, complained that the arts and sciences had made him unhappy, Merteuil and Valmont show that they can use them to make others unhappy. Their enlightenment buys them an advantage over those too young or ill-educated to match them. A mastery of the rhetoric of plays and sentimental novels helps to seduce the weak characters around them who then become the embodiments of scientific truths that Valmont and Merteuil observe, the objects of experiments that they conduct, the characters in the narratives that they construct.

The other characters are powerless in the face of such a frightening coincidence of intelligence and malice, and once Valmont and Merteuil are removed, their attempts to derive a morally edifying conclusion are feeble. When, for instance, Merteuil is struck down with smallpox, a moral conclusion is summoned and she is hurriedly and loudly declared to be the rightful victim. Mme de Volanges reports this news in letter 175 and quotes the observation of a Marquis who was present that 'à présent son âme était sur sa figure. Malheureusement tout le monde trouva que l'expression est juste' (at the moment her soul was on her face. Unfortunately everyone thought the expression apt). Volanges distances herself from this conclusion with her use of the adverb 'malheureuse-ment' suggesting that she, if not her society, has learned not to be impressed by glib equations of appearance and reality or by the 'bons mots' that reverberate around society. Her use of the present tense in ('l'expression *est* juste') suggests, however, that this is unlikely to change.

The appearance of this 'deus ex machina' (the term for a con-trived force that arrives suddenly at the end of a work to provide a resolution that otherwise seems elusive) ironically reassures those who have been frightened by this world of machinations and mate-rialism. They prefer to believe that writing is transparent and individual too, and that, as Danceny puts it (in letter 150) 'une lettre est le portrait de l'âme' (a letter is the portrait of the soul). Merteuil's soul is now there for all to see. Suddenly the antinomy of appearance and reality, things material and spiritual, is swept away. Earlier the moral outlook of the other characters depends on this collusion of inner and outer worlds. Volanges warns Tourvel of Valmont's misadventures: 'Je pourrais vous en raconter qui vous feraient frémir; mais *vos regards, purs comme votre âme*, seraient souillés par de semblables tableaux' (I could tell you some which would make you shudder; but your demeanour, pure as your soul, would be sullied by such pictures). The soul has an almost self-evi-dently physical existence. The machinations of Valmont and Merteuil have depended upon their victims believing that what they see is what they get, that there is an equivalence of appear-ance and reality. They should have learned that this is not the case. The folly which made the victory of Merteuil possible now explains her defeat. Or the remark suggests that this world remains more impressed by a display of wit than an effort to understand. If Rosemonde recommends more cautiously that we submit to the decrees of Providence without purporting to understand them, the concluding words of Danceny, as he leaves for the Knights of Malta (and the security of an unchanging chivalrous world, as do Des Grieux in *Manon Lescaut*, Déterville in Madame de Graffigny's *Lettres d'une Péruvienne* and Léon in Beaumarchais's *La Mère coupable*) perhaps shows the most convincing acquisition of good sense. As he writes to Rosemonde, having read Merteuil's letters (letter 174):

> Si vous les lisez, vous ne verrez peut-être pas sans étonnement qu'on puisse réunir tant d'ingénuité et tant de perfidie. C'est, au moins, ce qui m'a frappé le plus dans la dernière lecture que je viens d'en faire.

> (If you read them, you will perhaps not be surprised to see that one can combine so much ingenuity and perfidy. That is, at any rate, what struck me the most when I read them once again a moment ago.)

He has now learned to consider and anticipate the reactions of his interlocutor, to see malice and intelligence as possible bedfellows, but, above all, to reread his correspondence.

In many works, then as now, evil characters are almost invariably stupid and ugly. Marivaux's 'indigent philosophe' claims that most often 'les méchants sont les plus ignorants de tous les hommes' (evil people are the most ignorant of all). They are the antithesis of Enlightenment. That Bartholo in Beaumarchais's *Le Barbier de Séville* (1775) dislikes free thought is betrayed by his ugliness and age. But, as Diderot's *Neveu de Rameau* suggests, some people have a natural talent for evil which deserves respect, since it often seems to require more ability and creativity to be bad than to be good. This awareness is taken on board by writers in the later years. Beaumarchais, for instance, creates in the figure of Bégearss in the drama *La Mère coupable* (1792), an enemy of the Enlightenment who, unlike Bartholo earlier, is also a participant in and beneficiary of it. He is a schemer similar to Figaro who differs only in being malevolent. It is clear that the 'good' characters in *Les Liaisons dangereuses* either do not understand why they pursue the good they believe in or cannot properly be called good because such a commendation presupposes a capacity for evil and they simply do not have the ingenuity or the independence required by vice. Conversely, Merteuil and Valmont are governed by rational and ethical systems that are both deliberate and lucid. Mme de Volanges shudders that Valmont's 'conduite est le résultat de ses principes' (his conduct is the result of his principles), while in the closing letters Merteuil is equally condemned for the systematic rigour of her ethics.

Contrary to what might be thought, Sade's writings are likewise extremely ethical, in that a series of philosophical decrees often explains and authorises sexual licence. This can be clearly seen in *La Philosphie dans le boudoir*.

3. Marquis de Sade, *La Philosphie dans le boudoir, ou les instituteurs immoraux* (1795)

The most scandalous and compelling instance of the connivance of enlightenment and passion, principle and crimes, is to be found in the works of Donatien-Alphonse-François, marquis de Sade (1740-1814). Imprisoned in 1778 for sexual and financial irregularities, Sade was released in 1790, but imprisoned again during the Revolution, only narrowly spared the guillotine and finally consigned to prisons and asylums from 1801 to his death. In prison he wrote a large amount of works, in the form of philosophical treastises (like the *Dialogue entre un prêtre et un mourant*, 1782) but, more commonly, novels. In these works it is not always clear whether the often rigorous philosophical systems which are outlined respect or parody the methods of other philosophers. He uses the tools sharpened by the Enlightenment discourse to knock at the edifices it constructs. Rather than entertaining doubts about philosophy, his works can be considered more properly to be a supreme projection of many of its ideas, pursued, in a sort of *reductio ad absurdum* (absurd exaggeration), to their very limits.

In *La Philosophie dans le boudoir* philosophy has made it into the private domestic space which was widely thought appropriate for it in the eighteenth century. Indeed, the 'boudoir' is that ideal space lying between the *salon* and the bedroom. It therefore acts as the hinge, in characteristic eighteenth-century fashion, between the realm of philosophical conversation and that of love. The boudoir seems to be the space where pleasure and reason might be reconciled. In a series of pedagogical dialogues, *libertin* characters, like the ironically named Madame de Saint-Ange, deploy the ideas used to secure virtue and faith to act against it. These educational dialogues perhaps mock Rousseau's educational treatises, just as *Juliette, ou les prospérités du vice* (1797) undresses and exposes *Julie* (1761), Rousseau's virtuous heroine of that name. Dolmancé, the central male protagonist, expounds theories that justify behaviour which we now call sadistic, on account of Sade. He tries to assure his pupil that 'la cruauté n'est autre chose que l'énergie de l'homme que la civilisation n'a point encore corrompue' (cruelty in nothing but the energy of man that civilisation has not yet corrupted). Like so many eighteenth-century philosophers, Dolmancé looks to nature for his authority and finds that even murder may be legitimised:

> La destruction étant une des premières lois de la nature, rien de ce qui détruit ne saurait être un crime. Comment une action qui sert aussi bien la nature pourrait-elle jamais l'outrager? Cette destruction, dont l'homme se flatte, n'est d'ailleurs qu'une chimère; le meurtre n'est point une destruction; celui qui le commet ne fait que varier les formes;

> (Since destruction is one of the primary laws of nature, nothing that destroys could be construed as a crime. How can an action which serves nature as well as this ever offend it? This destruction, which man reckons he understands, is then a mere illusion; murder is not destruction; he who commits it is only changing the forms around;)

The exposition of these ideas is chilling, not only on account of the possible effects which they would unleash, if taken seriously, but of the deliberate tone with which they are presented. He does not authorise anarchy through instinct, but orders and controls passion through reason. Like a good eighteenth-century philosopher, Dolmancé consults the laws of nature, having acquainted himself with the philosophical methods and conclusions. Perhaps he has been eavesdropping on the conversations about theories of flux from a work such as *Le Rêve de d'Alembert* where forms, human and inanimate, feed into one another. Like a good unlearned eighteenth-century woman, his pupil Eugénie also duly responds as she should: 'je dois respecter des principes qui conduisent à des égarements' (I must respect principles which lead to aberrations). She remains aware of moral norms (hence she sees aberrations) but is more impressed by the force of principles that cut across them.

*

The Enlightenment authorises the mastery of one's environment and mastery soon permits destruction. Often basing his analyses on the work of Sade, the theorist Michel Foucault has argued that just when the triumph of reason seems most secure, unreason is invited back and enters into dialogue with it. Reason encounters its opposite in order to assure itself of its supremacy. The Enlightenment then does not secure happiness, but by making the connection between knowledge and power explicit, creates an environment which does not respect that which deviates from its principles. The hindsight of a bitter twentieth century has muted such optimism as we might find in the Enlightenment. Critics have seen the Enlightenment as the first unwitting but decisive step towards a culture which would subsequently permit the systematic destruction which took place in the Holocaust.

Selected Reading

Michel Foucault, *Histoire de la folie à l'age classique* (Paris: Gallimard, 1972). Known in the English translation as *Madness and Civilisation* (London: Routledge, 1989). An important work of theory which traces the way madness was treated in the eighteenth century in order to expose new dimensions to the age and its assumptions about human reason.

S. Harvey et al, eds, *Reappraisals of Rousseau: Studies in Honour of R.A. Leigh* (Manchester: Manchester University Press, 1980). A good, wide-ranging study of Rousseau.

Max Horkheimer and Theodor Adorno, *Dialectic of Enlightenment* (London: Allen Lane, 1973). One of the most influential statements to question the Enlightenment, heavily influenced by the experience of World War II, but still pertinent.

Reinhart Koselleck, *Critique and Crisis: Enlightenment and the Pathogenesis of Modern Society* (Berg, 1988). A challenging, influential study of political and philosophical tensions in the Enlightenment.

Colette V. Michael, ed. *Sade: His Ethics and Rhetoric,* (New York: Peter Lang, 1989). A wide-ranging set of essays devoted to questions of morality and language in Sade's works.

Ronald Rosbottom, *Choderlos de Laclos* (Boston: G.K. Hall, 1978). A good introduction to *Les Liaisons dangereuses.*

Jean Starobinski, *Transparency and Obstruction* (London; Chicago University Press, 1988). A classic study of Rousseau's unique predicaments and solutions which illuminate all his works.

V

Thought on Religion

The philosophical convictions of the eighteenth century in general presuppose a more positive view of human nature. The Enlightenment philosophers assert human beings as figures capable of standing tall and walking into the future. They also show that, irrespective of the particular goals to which they aspire, the pursuit of knowledge itself is validated. In contrast to Pascal's disdain for the *libido sciendi* (the lust for knowledge) they argue that knowledge should be both pleasurable and, Rousseau notwithstanding, useful. The tree of knowledge is cultivated once again and the Fall overcome, as Newton's apple (which epitomises gravitation) displaces Adam's (which encapsulates the idea of original sin). Most of the *philosophes* were hostile to Christianity in one way or another. But once the complex of Christian ideas and beliefs was eliminated, it was more difficult to agree on a viable system that was both intellectually plausible and morally secure. The *philosophes* found that they had merely jumped from the saucepan of Christian supremacy into the fire of belief systems such as materialism or determinism which left man with even less liberty. If the Enlightenment thinkers were largely opposed to Christian beliefs and traditions, it would be wrong to assume either that there was no serious Christian writing in the eighteenth century or that this was not itself aligned with many of the *philosophes*' ambitions and ideals. Fénelon, appointed archbishop of Cambrai in 1695, was a political exile from the court of Louis XIV, having written the most influential critique of his absolutism in *Télémaque*, which saw more reprints than any other book in the eighteenth century. Likewise, at the other end of the century, when Christianity, along with its calendar, had been suppressed by the Revolution, it proved possible for the figure of the abbé Grégoire (1750-1831) to fight for revolutionary values while retaining his episcopal function.

1. Christianity

The increasingly religious regime of Louis XIV (latterly under the influence of his second wife, the devout Madame de Maintenon, 1635-1719) had supported, and had been supported by, a number of extraordinary orators in the late seventeenth century. Jacques-Bénigne Bossuet and Pierre Bourdaloue, whose long sermons gave the name to a type of chamber pot to be used discreetly during them, were succeeded by Jean-Baptiste Massillon (1663-1742), who preached the funeral oration of Louis XIV in 1715. Massillon is an interesting figure because his rhetoric and his eloquence, however characteristic of the previous century, are the vehicle for ideas that are more palatable to the eighteenth century. In a set of sermons known as the *Petit Carême* preached, three years after Louis XIV's death, over Lent 1718 before the nine-year old Louis XV, Massillon seems to suggest that if the age of extravagant talent and absolute power was waning, this might be no bad thing. Massillon reminds the young Louis of the dependency of the 'grands' or the great men of the state on the modest lower strata of society:

> Toute puissance vient de Dieu, et tout ce qui vient de Dieu n'est établi que pour l'utilité des hommes. Les grands seraient inutiles sur la terre, s'il ne s'y trouvaient des pauvres et des malheureux; ils ne doivent leur élévation qu'aux besoins publics; et loin que les peuples soient faits pour eux, ils ne sont eux-mêmes tout ce qu'il sont que pour les peuples.

> (All power comes from God, and all that comes from God is established only for the utility of people. The grandees would be useless on earth, if there were no poor and unfortunate people there; they owe their elevated position to the public need; and far from people being made for them, they are themselves all that they are only for the people's benefit.)

Massillon first suggests that power comes from God and that the King is a divine representative, but proceeds to place more emphasis on his responsibility to the poor, arguing that the rich and poor are interdependent. On the Passion Sunday a little while later, Massillon goes further and depicts more graphically the dangers of despotism in a future tense which does not altogether allay suspicions that it is hiding the recent past under Louis XIV.

> Qu'est-ce qu'un souverain né avec une valeur bouillante, et dont les éclairs brillent déjà de toutes parts dès ses plus jeunes ans, si la crainte de Dieu ne le conduit et ne le modère? Un astre nouveau et malfaisant qui n'annonce que des calamités à la terre. Plus il croîtra dans cette science funeste, plus les misères publiques croîtront avec lui [...] il croira effacer par l'éclat de ses victoires leur témérité ou leur injustice [...] ses voisins deviendront ses ennemis dès qu'ils pourront devenir sa conquête; ses peuples eux-mêmes fourniront, de leurs larmes et de leur sang, la triste matière de ses triomphes.

> (What is a sovereign born with a burning valour whose flashes of brilliance light up all parts already in his youngest days, if the fear of God does not direct and moderate him? A new malignant star which announces only calamities to the earth. The more he grows in this fatal science, the more public misery increases with him [...] he will think he can cover up the temerity or the injustice of his victories by their brilliance [...] his neighbours will become his enemies as soon as they can become his conquests; his own people will furnish, with their tears and blood, the sorry material for his triumphs.)

The nouns readily associated with glory and brilliance, 'valeur', 'astre', even 'science', are all qualified by adjectives which debase them: 'bouillante', 'malfaisant', 'funeste'. After the initial allusion to God, Massillon evokes miseries on earth that result from belligerence and despotism. The imagery does not only assist the argument for the necessity of a Godfearing monarch but seems to grow into a self-sufficient condemnation of actual and specific injustices. With a pungency worthy of Voltaire, Massillon's sermons are animated by an interest in the plight of man rather than an insistence on dogma.

The increasingly dogmatic quality of Louis XIV's Catholicism had been announced in 1685 by the revocation of the edict of Nantes which had been set up in 1598 by Voltaire's hero, Henri IV. All dissenting religious groups, notably the Huguenots, were eliminated from France. State religion was henceforward widely associated with injustice and intolerance. Christian beliefs tended to be feared by Enlightenment writers as the most potent and dangerous form of irrationality, susceptible to becoming fanaticism. An uncomfortably recent history had been changed and scarred by the religiously motivated assassinations of Henri III (1589) and Henri IV (1610). Apparently inflamed by Jesuit propaganda, a man by the name of Jean-Louis Damiens attacked Louis XV in 1757, perhaps helping towards the eventual expulsion of the Jesuits from France in 1764. Haunted by such events, eighteenth-century writers who worried either that religion enjoyed inordinate influence in shaping or dictating the *status quo* or that it threatened to destroy it. But the traditional forms of religion remained important in stamping their influence on those who would later reject them. No important figure neglected to reflect on religion. Voltaire and Diderot were, like many free thinkers, brought up in Jesuit schools. Rousseau converted in and out of Catholicism. Although there remained much pious Christian literature, it had to turn increasingly to the urgent task of defending the Christian faith against the onslaught of the *philosophes*.

The most formidable alternative which Christianity had to face, at least in the earlier years of the century, was Deism. Deism answered the call for a religion which would not overheat but which could acclimatise to the temperate philosophical atmosphere of the age.

2. Deism

Deists sought to affirm God's existence by defending the rationality of religion and attacking the irrationality of Christian beliefs, especially miracles, which disturbed the universality and coherence of the universe that Newton had shown to be governed by mechanistic laws. God was viewed chiefly as the Creator who, having initiated and legislated matters, had let the universe run its course. God was worshipped as a clockmaker, because the world functioned like clockwork, or was conceptualised as a geometer. Deism was motivated both by a conviction that the natural world compels and declares our belief in such a God and that it suits the social world to do so too. The character of Deism depended chiefly on the particular blend of this enthusiasm and pragmatism. One of the fears that remained even among *libertin* circles is that, in the absence of religious belief, limitless self-interest would prevail and destroy us, for if God did not exist, man would become God, uninhibited in his designs on the world. Man should believe in God because all hell would break loose otherwise. As we hear in the seventeenth 'entretien' of Voltaire's dialogue *L'A.B.C* (1768):

> Je veux que mon procureur, mon tailleur, mes valets, ma femme même croient en Dieu; et je m'imagine que j'en serai moins volé et moins cocu.

> (I want my steward, my tailor, my servants and even my wife to believe in God; and I imagine that I will be less stolen from and less of a cuckold.)

This cynical, self-interested recommendation of belief in God is counteracted by his hint that belief in God does not entail absolute standards of virtue. The fact that he only imagines (rather than believes or hopes) he will be 'moins volé' and 'moins cocu' (rather than 'pas volé' and 'pas cocu') suggests that their faith in God will not spare him altogether the pain and ignominy of theft and cuckoldry. This statement raises another problem that haunts the Enlightenment even at its most urgently didactic. It voices the suspicion that everyone should believe in God apart from me. This epitomises the problem of prescribing virtue for others. In his arguments against supposedly moral plays in the *Lettre à d'Alembert*, Rousseau argues that we all love to applaud virtue, but none more so than the criminal who will thrive less if everyone else is criminal, and who finds the economy of particular vice and general virtue optimal.

In the *Lettres philosophiques*, commerce becomes the new means to take account of and regulate the indomitable assertions of the self. A love of money unites us. Self-love is what we all have in common. In the tenth letter of the *Lettres philosophiques* Voltaire makes the comparison between religion and commerce. By asserting our natural self-interest, our differences are made to look what they are; colourfully, even comically inessential.

Entrez dans la bourse de Londres... vous y voyez rassemblés les députés de toutes les nations pour l'Utilité des hommes. Là, le Juif, le Mahométan et le Chrétien traitent l'un avec l'autre comme s'ils étaient de la même Religion et ne donnent le nom d'infidèles qu'à ceux qui font banqueroute; [...] Au sortir de ces pacifiques et libres assemblées, les uns vont à la Synagogue, les autres vont boire; celui-ci va se faire baptiser dans une grande cuve au nom de Père par le Fils au Saint-Esprit; celui-là fait couper le prépuce de son fils et fait marmotter sur l'Enfant des paroles hébraïques qu'il n'entend point...

(Go into the London Stock Exchange... There you will see an assembly of all the nations for the utility of mankind. There, the Jews, the Mohammedans and the Christians trade with one another as if they were of the same religion and describe only those people who go bankrupt as infidels; [...] Upon leaving these peaceful and free assemblies, some go to the synagogue, others go to drink; this one goes to be baptised in a great bowl in the name of the Father, the Son and the Holy Ghost; that one goes to have the foreskin of his son cut and to have words of Hebrew murmured over the child which it does not understand.)

Credit has been said to be of more value than creeds. The German historian Meinecke called Voltaire the 'banker of the Enlightenment', referring not only to his defence of 'luxe' but his propensity to hoard the ideas of others. But his view of religion in this pragmatic light is shared by others. Beneath the dogma and the ceremonies, all religions and all people are motivated by the same assumptions and desires. Montesquieu's Persians remark in the *Lettres persanes* (1721) that all religions stem from the same 'souche' or root. The metaphor emphasises the natural dimension to religion which thinkers of the Enlightenment value. All religions rest on a common belief in truth and a desire to teach

morality. No-one therefore has a right to exclusive revelation. By
drawing the elements common to Christianity, Islam and Judaism,
he comes up with a deistic Creator-God. The Persians observe that
minority religions serve the economy well, since their energies are
diverted into industry and commerce.

Arguments for religion adduce the proof that it served the
nation. This pragmatic strain informs many arguments about religion. Voltaire eschews discussions of God versus the devil, or good
versus bad, but, rerouting such debates in social directions, they
become dialogues between believers and atheists, priests and
philosophers. Metaphysical discussions are exchanged for economic arguments. Monasteries are not good for an age of
decreasing demography. The philosophers care little for chastity.
Hobbes had argued that chastity was contrived by the papacy in
order to secure a patency for religion so that it might look distinct
from the dynastic structures of all other powers and therefore
bring to itself even greater influence.

De l'esprit des lois (1748) asserts that the religion of a given nation
is grounded in non-transcendental matters like the soil and climate. Led by Voltaire, many thinkers permitted and encouraged
the indulgence of self-interest as a force which was not noxious
and a good deal more compelling than religion. But those with a
more satirical bent not only asserted the rights of self-interest
against religion but argued that religion itself was a function of
self-interest. In other words, religion reflected our own preoccupations. With characteristic mischief, Voltaire remarks that God
made man in his own image and we returned it. Montesquieu's
Persians likewise reflect on the relativity of all perceptions. As Rica
writes,

> Il me semble, Usbek, que nous ne jugeons jamais des choses que par
> un retour secret que nous faisons sur nous-mêmes [...] On a dit fort
> bien que, si les triangles faisaient un dieu, ils lui donneraient trois
> côtés.
>
> (It seems to me, Usbek, that we only ever judge anything by making
> a secret return into ourselves... It has been said very rightly that if
> the triangles made a God, they would give him three sides.)

The conceit is innocuous enough, but perhaps it is charging the universally valid language of geometry (lauded by d'Alembert as the purest of all intellectual exercises) with the same self-regard and relativity. Here he is suggesting that even the geometric God of Deism is a function of our self-interest, but perhaps also it refers back to an earlier discussion concerning the Trinity, when the Persians remark that that the Pope can magically make one out of three. Rica's hypothesis about triangles uses the verb 'faire' (it would have been barely more hypothetical to say if triangles *believed* in a God or *had* a God) and thereby quietly makes sure that our imagination has an active part in constructing these Gods.

As the century progresses, the purely rational basis for faith tends to make way for a more emotional response. Faith can be anchored within a more affective or sentimental relationship. For all his infernal wit, Voltaire, it seems, believed passionately in his God. In Ferney there still stands the church on which is inscribed 'Deo erexit Voltaire' (Voltaire erected this to God). The rather impudent proximity of the names in this proclamation ensures the redundancy of priests in this deistic church. But the geometer's universe which is admired as a piece of craftsmanship becomes identified with our more specific experience of an agreeable natural world.

Rousseau's 'Profession de foi du vicaire savoyard' (the Savoyard vicar's profession of faith), in book four of *Emile* places the emphasis both on the outer world and the inner one of conscience. Again the exposition of ideas takes the form of a 'real' dialogue between a vicar and Emile which takes place with a particularly beautiful, mountainous scene as a backdrop: 'On eût dit que la nature étalait à nos yeux toute sa magnificence pour en offrir le texte à nos entretiens' (one might have said that nature displayed for our eyes all her magnificence to offer the text for our discussions). Instead of the traditional platform of a Biblical text cited at the opening of a sermon, nature's beauty is the immediate subject which motivates and directs the subsequent profession. The vicar professes a belief that God's truths are implanted in us. He therefore does not instruct Emile, but tells him where to look for these instructions. 'Et ce que Dieu veut qu'un homme fasse, il ne le lui fait pas dire par un autre homme, il le lui dit lui-même, il l'écrit au fond du coeur' (and what God wants a man to do, he does not have it said to him by another man, he writes it at the bottom of his heart). It is written and yet not so much read as seen, or rather sensed. The display of nature shows how moral and physical environments reflect one another. However, as important for Rousseau as the argument by design is the internal assent, an inner landscape invulnerable to the opinions outside it. In a reworking of Descartes, a sort of affective *cogito*, the self is its own judge: I feel, therefore it is:

> Je ne tire point ces règles des principes d'une haute philosophie, amis, je les trouve au fond de mon coeur écrites par la nature en caractères ineffaçables. Je n'ai qu'à me consulter sur ce que je veux faire; tout ce que je sens être bien est bien, tout ce que je sens être mal est mal.

> (I do not draw these rules from the principles of a profound philosophy, friends, I find them written at the bottom of my heart by nature in indelible letters. I have only to consult myself about that which I want; all that I feel is good is good, all that I feel is bad is bad.)

The language of the Savoyard vicar is beautifully simple, but he employs a metaphor characteristic of Rousseau when speaking of philosophical principles that are etched indelibly at the bottom of his heart. This image corresponds to the desire to find a language characterised by an inviolate and immediate inner truthfulness, where truth is not subject to the intrusive and misappropriating gaze of a reader, where knowledge is truly self-knowledge, where he feels what he knows and is what he writes, so that Rousseau can say, like Laclos's Merteuil, 'je suis mon ouvrage' (I am my own work).

The *Profession de foi* then adumbrates a religion based on a mixture of responses foreseen by the conscience and the will. Rousseau also places an emphasis not only on the influence of the natural world in shaping our sensibilities and our understanding of God but on the determinants of childhood and its importance in accounting for man's subsequent sentiments and beliefs.

Although Voltaire is, with reason, cast as the polar opposite of Rousseau, their expressions of deism, each tinged with pragmatism, in fact converge surprisingly. Rousseau himself opts in his *Contrat social* for what he calls a civil religion which guarantees social virtue. Even Voltaire, known for espousing the rational, pragmatic view in matters of faith epitomised in the much-quoted 'Si Dieu n'existait pas, il faudrait l'inventer' (if God did not exist it would be necessary to invent him), is capable of an emotional response to the Supreme Being that is predicated on nature. His late *conte*, the *Histoire de Jenni, dialogue entre un athée et un sage* (1775) makes explicit this basis for the faith. Like Rousseau, he tries to accede to a language that is immediate, a direct line between God and man. If God transmits his truths directly to the individual, Voltaire hopes that a return journey might be possible. Rousseau accuses Voltaire and all the other Enlightenment writers of merely addressing coteries and cabals and neglecting to develop a meaningful and trustworthy relationship between themselves and their readers. Rousseau tries to place the manuscript of his *Dialogues* onto the altar at Notre Dame in order to accede with all the immediacy possible to the truth. Voltaire concludes his *Traité sur la tolérance* with a prayer which indicates the same, if less frantic, desire to reach beyond human discourses to a truth that is immediate: 'Ce n'est plus aux hommes que je tourne, mais à vous que je m'adresse' (it is no longer to man that I turn, but only to you that I address these words). Voltaire's vision of religion is also a dream of immediacy beyond human discourse itself.

However, unlike Rousseau, Voltaire is committed to satirising and challenging religions in order to combat the abuses they support and the fanaticism which they foment. He becomes a crusader against organised religion, adept at borrowing its emotive power and its capacity to persuade and transform through allying ideas and passions. When celebrating Newton's miraculous physics, Voltaire redeploys a traditional lexicon in the interests of new science. A cuckoo in the clerical nest, Voltaire is himself mysteriously subject to a fever every year on the day of St. Bartholomew, such is his continuing horror at the atrocities committed against Protestants on that day in 1572. Fanaticism is a sort of contagion. Philosophy is the palliative to this poison. Voltaire, who admires the clarity and impact of Christ's sayings and parables, swings between imitation and parody of the style and emotions that inform religious discourse.

Deists then tend to argue for Religion as a need integral to our existence, and not just a social expedient. The existence of God allows us to understand or at least intuit our position in the world. Just as philosophy consists in great part of the apprehension of everyday phenomena, so religion chiefly entails a grateful sensibility to the world around. Descartes had argued that God must exist and from that deduced the necessity and centrality of thought. For deists it was the other way round: The universe looks as though it is the work of a creator and man in general behaves as though there were a God, so there must be one. However, there were those also who, looking about them, saw evil unleashed both by man and nature. These people were atheists.

3. Atheism

The increasing emotional investment in deism is perhaps attributable to the growing and, for many, menacing, presence of atheism which was widely seen to be as pernicious as fanaticism. By the 1770s atheism had begun to relegate deism, but it had simmered long before. In the seventeenth century, atheism was the badge of a certain *libertin* type, but Pierre Bayle had dignified it by suggesting in his *Dictionnaire historique et critique* (1697; 1702) that atheists could co-exist without destroying one another. He argued that for secular reasons they would survive.

It is, nevertheless, difficult for us now to imagine just how execrable and dangerous atheism was considered to be, even up to the French Revolution. The diffusion of heterodox ideas was often assured by clandestine works but achieved also by those works which tried to combat these ideas. For this reason, works against atheism, such as that by Antoine Louis Séguier (1726-92), could be prohibited. Many fictional works are able to advance dangerously subversive elements by subordinating them to an overall design that condemns them without all the force required to do so. The prudish remarks of the 'editor' and moral conclusions of Laclos's *Liaisons dangereuses* pale in comparison to the central characters and the intelligence they manifest. In *Les Infortunes de la vertu* (1787) Sade's moralising conclusion that 'le véritable bonheur n'est que dans le sein de la vertu' (true happiness is only to be found in the heart of virtue) is a self-consciously trite and hollow concession after the many transgressions of moral codes which precede it.

Diderot, whose early work testifies to a deistic faith, is again influential in turning deistic arguments on their head and lending credibility to atheistic arguments. Voltaire and Rousseau put their trust in vision: in Voltaire's case, the clear sight of an ordered universe; in Rousseau's case, the hazier prospect of natural beauty. Vision is prized beyond the languages in which we can express religion, but, unlike the projections of seers and visionaries, theirs is an empirical vision which informs us that we and the natural world in which we live are the only miracles. The claim voiced by Freind (the name is that of an English physician, but suggests more generally that he should be trusted) in Voltaire's *Histoire de Jenni* does not rely on sophisticated exegetical or philosophical argument: 'Pour savoir s'il est un Dieu, je ne vous demande qu'une chose, c'est d'ouvrir les yeux' (if you want to know whether there is a God, I ask you to do just one thing and that is to open your eyes).

Diderot's response in the *Lettre sur les aveugles* (1749) is devastating as it is simple. He stages a conversation between a dying blind mathematician, Professor Saunderson (1682-1739), and a minister by the name of Holmes to question the wisdom of beliefs in God which are predicated on the argument from design – the notion that the structure or design of the world indicates the touch of a Creator. Trying the tactic which works for Freind, Holmes asks Saunderson to see the God in the world around him. Holmes fails to detect that a blind man may require different criteria to sustain a belief in God. Saunderson needs to touch God in order to satisfy himself that God exists. Not only is the blind man unable to see the phenomena which sanction the existence of God for deists, but the fact that he cannot proves the fallibility and cruelty of the natural world. Saunderson proffers a more radical version of the deistic insight that God is a function of our preoccupations. Here it is implied, more disturbingly, that God is a function of our limitations. Deists, maintaining all the while that it is natural to believe in God, playfully suggest that the type of God, its extrinsic aspects of colour or form, are conditioned by our cultural prejudices. But here belief in God, rather than in particular aspects of God, is itself a product of these prejudices. And while deists believe that our cultural differences account for the various material forms which we lend this spiritual entity, it is now clear that it is our own material differences which produce Gods, even the abstract immaterial sort beloved of the deists.

The implication is not only that blind people inhabit a world of different signs and values and therefore will believe in a different God, but that the religious beliefs of people endowed with an apparently usual number of senses are also subject to this relativity. By definition humans could not know that they lacked further senses if they did. Were the configuration of our senses different we would believe in a different God. The blind man, far from lacking insight into these matters, is a sort of visionary. His words on the deathbed eclipse those of conventional discourse and lend him the same sort of transcendental aura that envelops the dreaming d'Alembert or the battered Belisarius.

Diderot is fascinated by deficiency and the possibilities offered by that which is underestimated or denounced by orthodox enlightenment discourse. These aberrations, known to the eighteenth century as 'monstres' (or monsters), were of course always a wide source of curiosity but now, promoted by such arguments as Diderot's, come to be considered as philosophically pertinent. Rather than admiring the static perfection of the geometric universe, we are bewildered by a spontaneously generated living nature as outlined in the *Rêve de d'Alembert*. John Turbervill Needham (1713-81), a contemporary of the great naturalist, the comte de Buffon (1707-88), had experimented with polyps and eels, concluding, as it happened wrongly, that spontaneous generation could take place and that creation could occur without the prompting of a creator. Fossilised shells had been found in the mountains, lending evidence to those who believed in primeval chaos, and provoking among those who did not the more modest suggestion that pilgrims had dropped their shells.

Many writers are inclined to fear that, in the absence of God, man would complete his own dreadful apotheosis. Whether it is an expression of man's redeeming dependency on the regard of others or, on the contrary, our overbearing and desperate self-importance, the afterlife now in greatest demand among the writers of the eighteenth century seems to be posterity. Atheism, however, chastens as much as it empowers. Atheists like Claude-Adrien Helvétius and the baron d'Holbach, whose *Système de la nature* (1770) was perhaps the century's most influential statement of atheism, removed not only the soul but free will from humans. Under the new and unpredictable stewardship of blind chance in an increasingly bizarre, impersonal world, man's dignity seemed jeopardised.

If the century begins, tentatively, to discuss what would happen if God did not exist, it now proceeds to ask what would happen if man did not exist. The answer takes at least two different forms. In a few cases, the new vision of nature's teeming resplendence affirms God even as it belittles or removes man. In his *Études sur la nature* (1784), Jacques-Henri Bernardin de Saint-Pierre deduces from the postulate that man is not necessary to the world an argument for the infinite perfection and generosity of the Supreme Being. But the other departure from this sense of a cosmos propelled by a genesis of its own envisages man as vulnerable to its materiality and flux, abandoned in a world which is changing and changing us; a world, in other words, where change is not the noble prerogative of enlightened reformers, but an inevitable dynamic in which we are but passive participants.

Selected Reading

Michael J. Buckley, *At the Origins of Modern Atheism* (Yale University Press, 1987). Includes comprehensive but readable chapters on Diderot and d'Holbach.

Bernard Cottret, *Le Christ des Lumières: Jésus de Newton à Voltaire 1680-1760* (Paris: Éditions du cerf, 1990). A very informative study of the impact on Christianity of eighteenth-century philosophers.

H. Daniel-Rops, *The Church in the Eighteenth Century* (London: Dent, 1964). An excellent survey with a healthy bias towards France, which discusses not only marginal religious groups and missionary activity, but the intellectual challenges faced by the Church.

Peter Gay, *Deism: An Anthology* (London; Princeton: Van Nostrand, 1968). A work largely concerned with English exponents of Deism, but contains a very useful introduction to the movement.

R.R. Palmer, *Catholics and Unbelievers in Eighteenth-Century France* (Princeton: Princeton University Press, 1939). Though now rather elderly, a book which discusses the Catholic orthodoxy and the central problems it faces in an equitable way.

Travel Accounts: Self and Other

In investigating the foundations of religion and the basis of Christianity, philosophers and writers of the eighteenth century often have recourse to travel. The inspection of other cultures allows the *philosophes* to measure the characteristics of certain religions against universal precepts, enabling them to identify that which is rational and that which can be consigned to the mass of heterogeneous and arbitrary phenomena which obstruct the course of reason. The eighteenth century is an age of travel for many other reasons. It is also the golden age for tourists, many on the Grand Tour (to the ancient sites largely in Italy) which was at its height, and this is reflected in the preoccupations of a great number and variety of texts. Their writers are sometimes led on imaginative and fictional journeys to different lands but they also weave their fictions around real places, inspired by the accounts of travellers who had visited them. From absolutist France exile compels as many journeys as curiosity induces, and curiosity is often sharpened by the rapacity of colonial interests.

Eighteenth-century writers become increasingly indignant and impassioned in exploring the injustices which characterise the slave trade. The first, tentative understanding of the exploitation which accompanies exploration and the desire to give the colonised other a voice is to be found in the baron de La Hontan's *Nouveaux voyages*, published in 1703. La Hontan, a French soldier who travelled with the colonial forces to Canada, tries to find terms other than the usual lazy and dismissive 'paysan' (peasant) for describing the cultures of the Hurons and the Algonquins and, in a dialogue with an Iroquois chief, allows the expression of views about the 'noble savage' and religion which will resonate later in the century, particularly in the *Histoire des deux Indes* (which sees its first edition in 1770), a great collaboration between Diderot, once again, and the abbé de Raynal.

Authors in the eighteenth century are aware of the different motivations for travel and rarely are their texts about foreign life not also pretexts for the expression of some home truths. In writing about a foreign culture they are as often commenting on their own. Moreover, writers taking their readers to utopias and distant lands become conscious of the fact that in committing their experiences, whether imagined or real, to words intelligible to a French audience they risk travestying them. The problems the self has understanding others are bound with the problems of language. The text is the means of mediating a form of understanding, but, it will be clear, it itself is an irredeemably European, artificial product. In short you need a new language to express new ideas. Travel accounts become such a highly popular form of entertainment in France that they seem to risk becoming reified in a genre bound by conventions and tastes that are particularly French. It becomes such a vogue that the further one travels the more one gratifies a fashion for this at home.

1. Montesquieu, *Lettres persanes* (1721)

The *Lettres persanes*, a 'succès de scandale' published anonymously in 1721, stages the arrival of two Persians, Usbek and Rica, in France, and the letters to and from Persia which follow both illuminate aspects of French life and exemplify the difficulty of learning through travel. The work ostensibly offers an ingenuous view of life in France which permits satirical insights about life at the court, religion and mores of all sorts. But it transcends satire to suggest relativities of a more universal kind. In letter VIII, Usbek explains that he has travelled to France because he has been exiled from Persia. His desire for truth and justice has made his presence there unacceptable and his exile inevitable. He explains portentously that his departure followed his frank demystification of sleaze in the Persian court:

> Dès que je connus le vice, je m'en éloignai; mais je m'en approchai
> ensuite pour le démasquer. Je portai la vérité jusques au pied du

trône: j'y parlai un langage jusqu'alors inconnu; je déconcertai la
flatterie, et j'étonnai en même temps les adorateurs et l'idole.

(As soon as I discovered vice, I distanced myself from it; but I then
approached it in order to unmask it. I carried the truth to the foot
of the throne: there I spoke a language hitherto unknown: I disconcerted flattery and I confounded at once the worshippers and
the idol.)

Like Rousseau's introduction to his first discourse this is an
impressive profession that the Enlightenment might want to
cherish, such is its concern for plain truths which reach the
spheres of political power and its abhorrence of any forms of flattery and duplicity. But, like Rousseau's introduction to the first
discourse, it is the prelude to a rather more equivocal understanding of right and wrong.

Usbek is met with the incredulous question 'Comment peut-on
être Persan? (how can one be a Persian?). The person making the
enquiry makes the mistake of starting from a normative 'on' that is
human nature as he knows it and assuming that Persians are some
sort of deviation from this basis. The Persian plain speaker, having
reminded himself thus of the candour which leads to his exile, proceeds to expose with masterful ingenuousness the curious
characteristics of France and shows how unnatural and deviant
from rational norms are the hegemony of its women, the superfi-
ciality of life in the capital and the corruption in the government
of the nation. These observations, motivated by the Republican
pen of Montesquieu, are all highly plausible and could belong to
the sort of moralistic discourse which is not uncommon in the age.
However, it gradually becomes clear that this paragon of honesty
and rectitude is indifferent to the injustices perpetrated in his
harem, when news of unrest there reaches him. In particular his
wife, Roxane, proves to have been grievously oppressed by Usbek
and is held in captivity by a team of eunuchs. For all his perspi-
cacity and satirical acumen, he fails to see, let alone respond to
patent injustices in his own conduct. The vehicle of the satire
becomes its object.

It is apparent then that the exiled Usbek was no typical Persian and yet it is he and not his companion Rica who now guards most jealously his adherence to and belief in Persian customs and truths. While Rica integrates into Parisian life and indeed eventually dresses as a Frenchman, Usbek remains more sharply critical of the Parisian *modus vivendi.* In fact, travel to France confirms his Persianness. The unlikely answer to the question 'où' or perhaps 'quand peut-on être persan?' (where/when can one be a Persian?) would seem to be 'abroad' in Usbek's case at least.

If Usbek thought he had spoken a new language at the Persian court from which he is exiled, he has another thing coming. Roxane has a 'langage nouveau' of her own and she speaks it triumphantly in the final letter of the novel. She now lists her own accomplishments in defying the status quo: 'j'ai séduit tes eunuques, je me suis jouée de ta jalousie, et j'ai su, de ton affreux sérail, faire un lieu de délices et de plaisirs, (I have seduced your eunuchs, I have cheated your jealousy and from within your awful harem, I have been able to make a place of delights and pleasures). She finally adds 'Ce langage, sans doute, te paraît nouveau' (this language, no doubt, appears new to you) before dying.

This allusion echoes and overcomes the 'langage nouveau' pronounced by Usbek. Her suicide completes another irony, for Usbek had earlier championed the right to suicide, in opposition to the laws of the Christian Church. One suspects he might not approve of this particular instance. Or, with further tragic irony, is her own gesture of defiance merely derivative of his since the achievement of her individuality takes place in eerily similar terms to his? She is tragically doomed to repeat Usbek's conception. She is obliged in her gesture of defiance to use terms already prefigured by her oppressor. The 'paraître' of her 'ce langage te paraît nouveau' is unfortunately apt. Even in affirming her innovation, she is falling into a cliché which we may remember Usbek uttering.

At all events the novel seems to raise the question of its own efficacy by exploring the limitations of these 'new languages'. Usbek fails to learn anything from his new experiences, keen as he is to observe them discriminately, while our own capacity to be challenged by any of the text's insights is in turn questioned. Does it merely gratify the sense of closure expected of the epistolary novel? The novel brings into play a variety of windows and mirrors only to suggest that we do not see ourselves in observing the problems of others. As Rica puts it in letter 52, 'ne sentirons-nous jamais que le ridicule des autres?' (will we only ever sense how ridiculous others are?) or that we see only ourselves and our own interests when trying to apprehend the other. As Rica says, 'nous ne jugeons jamais des choses que par un retour secret que nous faisons sur nous-mêmes' (we only ever judge anything by making a secret return into ourselves).

The *Lettres persanes* is beautifully construed around symmetries and resonances and is cemented by ironies in an attempt to please us rather than inform us about Persia and its inhabitants. The preface authenticates itself, in good eighteenth-century fashion, by claiming that the work is a translation from a genuine collection of Persian letters. Again the desire to authenticate the story it tells merely confirms the fabrication inherent to language. It itself resists the idea of a new language. Written in the French which convention demands, the text has been diluted in a translation.

> Je ne fais donc que l'office du traducteur: toute ma peine a été de mettre l'ouvrage à nos moeurs. J'ai soulagé le lecteur du langage asiatique autant que je l'ai pu, et l'ai sauvé d'une infinité d'expressions sublimes, qui l'auraient envoyé jusque dans les nues.

> (My job is only that of translator: I have put all my efforts into making the work acceptable to our customs. I have relieved the reader of the Asian language as much as I could and have saved the reader from an infinite number of sublime expressions which would have transported him into the clouds.)

The exchange between different cultural experiences projected by the Persians' journey to France has been taxed by language. The notions of relief and salvation to which the translator alludes suggests that he panders to a hyperbolic fear of the culture which he wishes to mediate, while the manner with which he describes the excesses of Persian expressions ironically betrays a similar hyperbole in French terms. Prejudice is already discernible in the apparently humble exercise of translation. Language stretches between the readers and the experience they read about. In the deistic dream of immediacy man dispenses with the revelation of scripture but here the desire for *prima facie* experiences of the world is occluded as it is mediated by the translation.

The reader of Voltaire's *contes* is not saved from the elaborate images and excesses of the oriental style with which *Zadig* for instance begins. Into the clouds we drift: 'Charme de mes prunelles, tourment des coeurs, lumière de l'esprit, je ne baise point la poussière de vos pieds. [...]' (charm of my eyelashes, tormentor of hearts, light of intelligence, I do not kiss the dust under your feet). The translator treats us to oriental stultiloquence at its best so we are mightily relieved to hear not long after that the hero Zadig quite simply 'se contentait d'avoir le style de la raison' (contented himself with having the style of reason). The subordination of whimsical exotic detail to a unitary rational truth is typical of Voltaire's writing. Many of the *contes* take us on a tour of exotic spots inhabited by Brahmins, Turkish philosophers and aliens from outer space. But all these seem to confirm an archetype of the rational philosopher. Travel accommodates the ingenuousness of the man who learns but it indulges the complacency of the philosopher whose wisdom is confirmed. The fondness for differences and idiosyncrasies is met by an implicit norm by which these are measured and from which they are seen to deviate. The confusion of the characters is offset by the ironic collusion of author and reader. As Roland Barthes says in his essay, *Le Dernier des écrivains heureux*, the journeys amount to an inspection of the philosopher's property. None of the characters challenge the fundamental assumptions of Voltaire's reason. We can in fact look closer at home for the extraordinary, exotic phenomenon which cedes to rational common sense for it is in the *Lettres philosophiques* that Voltaire most brilliantly uses travel to foreign climes to drive home philosophical points.

2. Voltaire, *Lettres sur les Anglais* or *Lettres philosophiques* (1734)

In an unlikely move calculated to upset preconceptions about his destination and its values (just as his final chapter on China in the *Siècle de Louis XIV* unsettles ideas about the century of Louis XIV),

Voltaire begins the letters he despatches from England with a discussion of Quakers. Voltaire himself begins by marvelling in this first letter at the phenomenon of the Quakers embodied in a curious chap he meets: 'J'ai cru que la doctrine et l'histoire d'un Peuple si extraordinaire méritaient la curiosité d'un homme raisonnable' (I thought that the doctrine and the history of such an extraordinary people would merit the curiosity of a reasonable man). The somewhat tentative 'j'ai cru' and the designation of his reader as reasonable fellow align us within a rather civilised epistolary perspective from which we can safely enjoy these phenomena that are heralded by the narrator not only as extraordinary but 'si extraordinaire', *so* extraordinary. A normative and civilised 'on' meets a bizarre, recalcitrant other, as it does when the Persians are asked 'comment peut-on être Persan?'. But of course as we read on it is the Quaker who is moderate and temperate and his people who can be called reasonable. Voltaire or his persona is duly exposed as contradictory and unreasonable. First, once they meet, we behold the polite and precious posturing of the Frenchman: 'Monsieur, lui dis-je, en me courbant le corps et en glissant un pied vers lui, selon notre coutume' (Sir, I said to him, while arching my body and sliding a foot towards him, as is our custom). It looks faintly ridiculous when compared to the gruff Quaker, but the veneer of politeness over the self-satisfaction is all the more thin. The next address is already more patronising as well as normative, 'mon homme', (my good man), 'cet homme singulier' (this singular man). When the Quaker admits that he is not baptised, Voltaire sounds like a furious, if old-fashioned French lorry driver. Suddenly imprecations follow the genuflections: 'Comment, morbleu, repris-je, vous n'êtes donc Chrétien' (what, gadzooks, I resumed, you're not a Christian then). And later, even better, he exclaims 'ventrebleu!' (zounds!). These words, at odds with the initially polite gestures, may well persuade us to revise our decisions about who is reasonable and who is outlandish. The exposition of Quaker beliefs takes place entirely in a conversation in which the tables are slowly but dramatically turned. The ostensible form of the letter gives way to a more emphatic, didactic tone. A somewhat anodyne opening deludes us. This same dynamic is discernible when Voltaire, having expounded matters of Christian doctrine, now undertakes to compare the merits of Newton and Descartes. He ensures likewise that this potentially abstruse discussion is the object of the same innocent and delighted curiosity. He begins the fourteenth letter, 'On Descartes and Newton', with the following report:

> Un Français qui arrive à Londres trouve les choses bien changées en Philosophie comme dans tout le reste. Il a laissé le monde plein; il le trouve vide. A Paris, on voit l'univers composé de tourbillons de matière subtile; à Londres on ne voit rien de cela. Chez nous c'est la pression de la Lune qui cause le flux de la mer; chez les Anglais, c'est la mer qui gravite vers la lune [...] A Paris, vous vous figurez la terre faite comme un melon; à Londres elle est aplatie des deux côtés.

> (A Frenchman arriving in London finds things very different in Philosophy as in all else. He has left the world full; he now finds it empty. In Paris the universe is made up of turbulences of subtle matter; in London none of this is to be seen. Back at home in France it's the pressure of the moon which causes the flux of the sea; in England it's the sea which gravitates towards the moon [...] In Paris you envisage the earth as though it's a melon; in London it is flattened at both poles.)

One might have thought that, like mathematics, philosophy would be the same everywhere, but it is apparently not so. Voltaire's style lends credibility to both systems so that the mutually exclusive cosmologies of Descartes and Newton are made to look like regional differences. These fundamentally divergent systems are reported with the curiosity of someone noting an arbitrary fact such as the side of the road we drive on. Voltaire does not begin to suggest that one system is and has to be wrong, but defers equitably to both. Indeed, the differences are made to look as though they are real. The terms, 'on trouve' and 'on voit' lend an empirical indubitability to what is related. This is amplified by the iterated 'c'est' as though England and France *are* different universes. Through the register of the travel book the amused traveller lulls the reader into accepting an exposition of Newtonian science, for Voltaire is clear that Descartes is actually wrong and Newton is right. If we look carefully at the passage, the almost imperceptible switch of Voltaire's allegiances can be glimpsed and the sense that these allegiances are determined by the veracity of each system. First, he is the amused, bemused tourist writing back home. 'Chez nous' allies writer and reader in opposition to the English mores. But within a few lines he has moved into the second person. The 'vous vous figurez' quietly indicates that you are wrong, in contrast with the factual observation relating to England. Voltaire occupies an indeterminate position. The brilliance and subtlety of the writing and the prejudices it seems initially to indulge make for a telling mediation of doctrinal and philosophical ideas. From an indeterminate position poised between England and France and in letters published at once in French and English, Voltaire channels truths so that the apparently bizarre or extraordinary phenomenon is finally subordinated to a reason that is universal, and what appear to be letters give way to a more monologic exposition.

Another work which explores new horizons in a self-critical manner is Diderot's *Supplément au voyage de Bougainville*, a work written about 1772 and published posthumously in 1798. This time the travellers are European. The explorer, Count Louis Antoine de Bougainville, had arrived at Hitia´a on Tahiti in April, 1768 and, after christening the island 'La nouvelle Cythère', had his journals published. Cythera, according to mythology the birthplace of Venus, was probably so called because the explorers came to observe the Transit of Venus, but it soon becomes clear that the myths of Venus, the Goddess of love, are also explored here. The moral and scientific certainties of the Enlightenment are embarrassed by questions of sexuality. The deputation of Frenchmen who disembark on the island are greeted by an eloquent spokesman for Tahitian culture by the name of Orou. He invites the 'aumônier' or chaplain, with traditional Tahitian hospitality, to bed with his daughters. The chaplain cannot quite say why it is wrong for him to do so. Orou exposes the folly of Western customs by entertaining other views of sexuality. Given the flux of the world to which they are naturally more sensitive, the Tahitians expose the morality of the Europeans, in particular the fidelity asked of them, as immobile and stifling.

However, like the *Lettres persanes*, the text is not merely a paean to foreign views of the world. It is clear that the natives are those who resist change and they show no reciprocal interest in the conventions of the French or any desire to learn from them. Their treatment of sterile women, for instance, seems no less oppressive. Europeans, for better or for worse, are more interested in the other. However, merely by virtue of looking at the world we are changing it. Just as Usbek mentions the case of a woman who limps when she notices people looking at her, so the gaze of the European is not innocuous. Moreover, as in the *Lettres persanes*, even if the gaze is innocuous, the terms into which this is translated and immobilised are not. After the 'adieux du vieillard', an old man's peroration about the benefits of nature accompanied by the symphonic sounds of breezes and the sea, A, one of the interlocutors, remarks sceptically: 'Ce discours me paraît véhément; mais à travers je ne sais quoi d'abrupt et de sauvage, il me semble retrouver des idées et des tournures européennes' (this discourse sounds vehement to me; but through whatever all this odd abrupt and wild stuff is, I seem to be able to find European ideas and turns of phrase). He is then reminded that this work has been translated twice over, from Tahitian to Spanish and then into French. Like many other eighteenth-century works, the text has already passed through several hands before it reaches ours. The exotic phenomena are couched in the idioms of an urbane French conversation. The Enlightenment ideal of transmitting into intelligible form philosophical ideas is itself threatened by the facility of that form. The immediate experience related by the translation is again self-consciously tenuous. There is something a little too comfortable and domestic about this 'tour de l'univers sur notre parquet' (the tour of the universe on our floor) as the work is described.

Rousseau considers these problems in his own way. In 'Des voyages' in book five of *Emile* (1762) he questions the utility of travel books and the effects of their extraordinary success in France:

> De tous les siècles de littérature, il n'y en a point où on lut tant que dans celui-ci, et point où l'on fut moins savant; de tous les pays de l'Europe, il n'y en a point où l'on imprime tant d'histoires, de rela-

tions de voyages qu'en France, et point où l'on connaisse moins le
génie et les moeurs des autres nations [...] En comparant le peu
que je pouvais observer avec ce que j'avais lu, j'ai fini par laisser là
les voyageurs, et regretter le temps que j'avais donné pour m'in-
struire à leur lecture, bien convaincu qu'en fait d'observations de
tout espèce il ne faut pas lire, il faut voir.

(Of all the ages which have produced literature, there have been
none which have read as much as this one and where people were
less knowledgeable; of all the nations of Europe, there is not one
which publishes so many histories and travel accounts as France and
where the character and manners of the other nations are less well-
known [...] In comparing the little that I have been able to observe
with that which I have read, I have ended up by leaving behind these
travellers and regretting the time I spent trying to educate myself in
reading them, convinced that when it comes to observations of all
kinds one must not read, one must see.)

Travel, contends Rousseau, is infinitely superior to travel books,
which are still only books. Parson Adams, the scholarly clergyman
in Fielding's *Joseph Andrews* (1742), expresses a caricatural, but
probably not unknown, disdain for travel when he asserts that
books represent 'the only way of travelling by which any knowledge
is to be acquired'. Indeed, Rousseau complains that the vogue for
travel books exempts us from travel. It does not enhance a sensitivity to nature and the world around us but only replaces this
experience with a nefariously vicarious existence. In other words,
it remains tainted by its literary connections. Although Rousseau is
more trenchant, the anxiety that travel literature is derivative and
familiar is itself implicitly visible in the works of those writing it.
The satisfaction that eighteenth-century France enjoys the most
vigorous and voracious readership creates anxieties of its own.
Travel accounts become clichés.

It is also patently clear from the texture of the passage above
and Rousseau's writing elsewhere that he can write as elegantly and
persuasively as the most committed author. The manipulation of
the paradox, the iterated 'où' with its crescendo up to the final
monosyllabic imperative, all remind us why he was known as

'Rousseau the eloquent'. Rather than abandoning the world of reading for that of seeing, Rousseau tries to combine the sensation of travel in the world with that of reading. It is apparent from the previous philosophical texts that Rousseau is indebted to the very rational, rhetorical forms that he condemns. Rousseau can only use texts to expose the folly of texts just as his opposition to reason is confirmed by reason itself. Rousseau throughout his work seeks to find in the evil itself its own panacea, and writing will compensate for the dangers of writing. In the *Confessions* (written between 1764 and 1770, published posthumously) and above all the *Rêveries du promeneur solitaire* (published posthumously in 1782) he tries to synthesise the motions of travel with the rhythms of his writing and show that they need not be at odds.

3. Rousseau, *Les Rêveries du promeneur solitaire* (1778)

'Tout est bien en sortant des mains de l'Auteur des choses, tout dégénère entre les mains de l'homme' (all is good when it leaves the hands of the Author of all things, all degenerates in the hands of man). The first lines of *Emile*, Rousseau's treatise on education which rehearses some of the ideas in the discourses and *Du contrat social*, guide us to the core of Rousseau's belief that humans are responsible for the degradation of God's designs in this world so all that is wrong is accountable to the corrupting influence of human agency. This line points us metaphorically to the concomitant difficulty. In Rousseau's image, transmission and corruption of these 'things' is effected between different pairs of hands. The image therefore attenuates the sweeping metaphysical pronouncement and evokes the problem of what happens when a book is passed from writer to reader, from 'auteur' to 'homme'. A text falls into a vacuum of interpretation. Rousseau was highly anxious that books could not be relied on to transmit securely a message. Rousseau is characterised by the unique tendency to sign his books in an attempt to effect a new intimacy between writer, text and reader. Alone among eighteenth-century writers, Rousseau is known pre-eminently by his first name, Jean-Jacques.

   Rousseau's travel is desultory, inward-looking, circular, languorous. He tries in the *Confessions* and *Rêveries du promeneur solitaire* to make writing respond to the rhythms of travel. His chapters, which he calls 'promenades', resemble the contours of a circuitous walk. Rousseau's thoughts and reminiscences are structured by the promenade, particular excursions which provoke associated reflections. The reverie is preferable to thought in that it does not presuppose an object as reflection or even dreams might. Such objects as the reverie commands present themselves. Writing is therefore like walking. Different pictures and features enter Rousseau's mental landscape.

The *Rêveries* vibrate continually between the 'lire' and the 'voir', the mediate and the immediate, the human and the natural, with an awareness of the problems that face travel writing he discussed in *Emile*. In a beautiful passage in the second promenade Rousseau describes how he is knocked over and out by a rampant Great Dane. Where others might have sued the owner, Rousseau exults in the loss of memory that results. Now more than ever, he enjoys being the underdog, for the boundaries of the self have been breached and for a few rapturous moments, Rousseau experiences the self immersed in and indivisible from greater phenomena. However, the following lines reinstate the presence of the self in all its fragile relativity, its fallible physicality, as Jean-Jacques hobbles back home. His wife is shocked by how disfigured he is. Rousseau then reports that exaggerated stories of his death at the paws of the dog have been circulating. The truth too has been disfigured: 'cette histoire se répandait dans Paris tellement chargée et défigurée' (this story spread around Paris in such an exaggerated and distorted way). Rousseau then follows this account with three further accounts of rumours or 'bruits' that echo and amplify the disfigurement that Rousseau experiences upon his return to himself from the dead. 'Bruits' disfigure him as painfully as his accident. The real scars are the outer equivalent of the injuries to his texts and the wounds these have caused him. The self is recuperated when he is asked upon his return, what his name and his address are. It is a self anchored by inessential co-ordinates, at odds with an intrinsic sense of self. The promenades of the *Rêveries* launch further voyages in search of a perfect selfhood, untrammelled and invisible to the gaze of the other, seeking paradoxically a sort of death where the self can be whole. The self eschews the dangers of self-portrayal for the security and plenitude of self-effacement. Travel and the writing of it then are forms of escapism. But Rousseau is too honest to the ambivalences of the self in travel and writing to be able to escape. He wanders on another occasion into a wild thicket where he appears to lose himself utterly, thereby regaining a sense of the original natural man that his second discourse had located. Or so it seems:

Je me comparais à ces grands voyageurs qui découvrent une île déserte [...] je me regardais presque comme un autre Colomb. Tandis que je me pavanais dans cette idée, j'entendis peu loin de moi un certain cliquetis que je crus reconnaître; j'écoute: le même bruit se répète et se multiplie. Surpris et curieux je me lève, je perce à travers un fourré de broussailles du côté d'où venait le bruit, et dans une combe à vingt pas du lieu meme où je croyais être parvenu le premier j'aperçois une manufacture de bas.

(I was comparing myself to one of those great voyagers who discover a deserted island [...] I saw myself almost as another Columbus. While I was wandering about with this idea, I heard at a little distance from me a certain clanking that I thought I recognised; I prick up my ears: the same noise repeats and multiplies itself. Surprised and curious I get up, I cut through a thicket of bushes where the noise was coming from and in a clearing not twenty paces from the very place where I thought I was the first ever to set foot I notice a stocking factory.)

Rousseau does not let the bathos, the 'bas' after the lyrically 'haut sublime', pass him by. It is an unusually comic moment, amplified by the long cumulative preceding sentence which abounds with adjectives. The machine introduces a version of the multiple 'bruits' that disfigured the truth and announced his return to human life. He comes back to earth. It is of course not only the machine, but its products, the stockings (somehow Rousseau knows a stocking factory instantly when he sees one) which suddenly announce the ubiquitously human, triumphant in its artifice and mediocrity. Rousseau is punished for thinking that he can be Columbus. Rousseau too cannot resist the temptation of the voyage and the discoveries it permits. Columbus is an enviable figure who reaches places where no-one has ever been, much like the hero of *Robinson Crusoe*, which is about the only reading he recommends for children in *Emile*. But once again the dream of commanding and innovating in the century is restrained by a sense of coming after. In fact, the terms on which his imagination asserts itself already restrict its possibilities (seeing himself as 'presque un autre Colomb' is more tentative than seeing himself as 'Colomb'), and his attempt to append a distinctive personal sense of himself to a historical, vicarious experience comes crashing down. The characters or writers themselves are painfully aware of having to live in a language that prefigures them, that is always trying to catch up with the experiences of the past.

Rousseau's reaction to the sudden sight of a stocking factory in the middle of nowhere is itself rather surprising. He explains that it provokes an 'agitation confuse et contradictoire' (a confused and contradictory disquiet) in that he is instinctively pleased to find evidence of human life in nature. In the *Rêveries* there results a new, acquiescent, even exhilarated sense of the duality that inhabits man who is unable ever to be himself. Rousseau now finds a delicious calm in the double existence conferred by reading which evokes both the memories of an event and the writing of that event. The memory of a walk is thus woken up again. He can therefore claim that 'la douceur que je goûte à les écrire doublera pour ainsi dire mon existence' (the pleasure which I take in writing them will double, so to speak, my existence). Writing then multiplies the self in a way that is ultimately not necessarily pernicious. It allows a privileged access to a world of the past, be it a mythical or a personal past, which can be relived. Writing is its own cure. Just as the vicar of the *Profession de foi* envisages letters inscribed deep in his heart, so he explains that the prize awarded by the Dijon academy can likewise be found 'au fond de mon coeur'. Virtue is described at the end of the first discourse as 'la science sublime' (the sublime science) or 'la véritable philosophie' (the true philosophy). Rousseau recycles negative terms of the language. Towards the end of the *Rêveries* for example he talks about the way his memories form a 'chaîne des idées accessoires' (chain of accessory ideas). It has been observed that the chains that fetter man at the opening of *Du contrat social* and those decorated by the garlands of the sciences and the arts in the first discourse have now modulated.

These forms of compensation structure Rousseau's thought in different ways. It is the basis for the *Confessions* in which a fictional self absolves the actual self writing it. That which needs to be confessed is redeemed by being repeated. Equally, *Du contrat social* envisages the lack of freedom in society compensated by further and in fact total removal of all natural autonomy to induce a more profound liberty. St Preux and Julie in Rousseau's *Julie* likewise give up love but are compensated by a higher dignity. Solitude has its compensations and allows a sense of one's fundamental nature and not the estrangement from oneself that relationships with others necessitate. In the *Rêveries* Rousseau finally finds in language a compensatory balm to the problems it began, restoring him to a sense of himself. Voltaire admonishes Rousseau for his tendency to 'écrire pour écrire', but the accusation can perhaps be corrected to 'j'écris pour sentir' (I write in order to feel). In the sinuous, poetic prose of his French, Rousseau at last finds an elusive 'langage nouveau' (new language).

The painful gap between text and nature, self and the world it is observing, is closed in these happier moments by the agency of writing. Rousseau's attempts to celebrate in language an intimate sense of the self in the world are echoed in the work of one of his most loyal disciples, Jacques-Henri Bernardin de Saint-Pierre, author of the *Études de la nature*.

4. Jacques-Henri Bernardin de Saint-Pierre, *Paul et Virginie* (1788)

The short story, *Paul et Virginie*, published first in volume four of the third edition of the *Études de la nature* in 1788, sits alongside more philosophical studies of nature and reminds us of the proximity of fiction and philosophy in the eighteenth century. Bernardin de Saint-Pierre makes the point, however, that the affective truths of the novel are of a different order to those embodied by history and the sciences. The novel is not to be sneered at as a mere fiction. *Paul et Virginie* is a poignant and earnest attempt to understand and evoke nature's beneficial properties. The story, a sort of eighteenth-century version of *Tarzan*, testifies tragically to the gap between nature and society suggesting that the economies particular to them are irreconcilable. Paul and Virginie are exemplary lovers who live blissful lives on the island of Île de France (now Mauritius) having grown up as if brother and sister. They live under a benign matriarchy, the women who preside over the little society having been forced to leave France because of scandals concerning the illegitimate birth of the children. Although they are from opposite ends of the social scale they achieve harmony and happiness in this new world. However, money shatters this idyll when Virginie is persuaded to return to France by her great-Aunt for financial reasons. She decides, however, that she will marry Paul (who has learned to read and write so he may correspond with her) and no-one else. Virginie returns. With a disaster prefigured by her name, she prefers modesty to security, indeed life itself, for, when her ship gets into trouble off the coast of the island, she refuses to remove her clothes and jump into the sea. Whereas the conflict between nature and society, exotic other and European self is predicated on a battle of virtue and vice, here it is clear that it is a western virtue, chastity, and not a vice, that leads to the conflict. Like Rousseau's Julie, Virginie is riven by two competing systems which do not allow her to be a woman compatible at once with nature and society. *Paul et Virginie* illustrates the Rousseauesque point that, while it would have been desirable to remain in the state of nature, it would be morally more dubious and dangerous to return to this Eden.

If the clash between cultures is tragic, the means of understanding this clash is more optimistic. Bernardin tries to show how nature and novel might be mapped onto one another. For a start, Bernardin enjoys painting nature in all its exotic colours, and the text tries to capture the beauty of the scene for the reader. But it is clear from the opening descriptive paragraph that this nature is not savage and undomesticated:

> Sur le côté oriental de la montagne qui s'élève derrière le Port-Louis de l'île de France, on voit, dans un terrain jadis cultivé, les ruines de deux petites cabanes. Elles sont situées presque au milieu d'un bassin formé par de grand rochers, qui n'a qu'une seule ouver-

ture, tournée au nord. On aperçoit à gauche la montagne appelée
le morne de la Découverte, d'où l'on signale les vaisseaux qui abor-
dent dans l'île, et, au bas de cette montagne, la ville nommée le
Port-Louis; à droite, le chemin qui mène du Port-Louis au quartier
des Pamplemousses; ensuite l'église de ce nom [...] On distingue
devant soi sur les bords de la mer la baie du Tombeau; un peu sur
la droite le cap Malheureux.

(On the eastern side of the mountain which rises behind Port-Louis
on the Île de France can be seen, on some land which was once cultivated, the ruins of two small huts. They are situated almost in the
middle of a basin formed by large rocks, which has only one
opening, facing the north. On the left can be seen the mountain
called the mount of discovery, from where ships approaching the
island are signalled to, and at the foot of this mountain, the town
called Port-Louis; on the right, the route which leads from Port-
Louis to the quarter of the Grapefruits; then the church of this
name [...] In front you can make out the Bay of the Tomb; a little
to the right the Cape of Misfortune.)

This passage does not appear to advance the plot and seems to
act primarily as a source of picturesque colour. But it has an important role in setting out the beliefs or ideals that inform this text.
Rather than evoking a wild and untamed environment it is
apparent, from the description of the church and the ships, that
this idyll is a blend of nature and civilisation. But what is perhaps
more striking is that the vision of this scene is inseparable from the
proper nouns that have been lent to describe its parts. Besides
evoking French colonial names in this wild paradise, the sites are
related to the events of the story. In fact it is, under the guise of this
description, already pointing to the plot. Places are anthropomor-
phised. Nature allows us to understand our own emotions while we
understand nature by appropriating it to our emotional experiences. This passage points us with foreboding to the misfortune
that has occurred (with its inauspicious description of ruins) but it
also seems to contain within it the solution.

This point is underscored when the narrator is seen etching
inscriptions from the Classics on trees. Nature herself is made leg-

ible. Texts are then not obstacles to an immediate experience of nature but are our access to it. Texts do not betray or misappropriate. As the narrator explains to Paul, 'un bon livre est un bon ami' (a good book is a good friend). The text is essentially trustworthy. Bernardin does not share Rousseau's paranoia that the book is a betrayal of the self. There is an absence of irony in the author's recommendation of the book's capacity, 'je me suis proposé de grands desseins dans ce petit ouvrage' (I have proposed great designs in this little work), which characterises it as the opposite of the more self-conscious *Supplément au voyage de Bougainville* which promised us a 'tour de l'univers sur notre parquet'. The text is then at once a vehicle for appreciating the most exotic landscapes and conveying the common humanity of feeling, of uniting the 'lire' and the 'voir' that were sundered in texts as Rousseau saw it. We should not be surprised that someone with as sharply ironic sensibilities as Flaubert should see to it in 1857 that Emma Bovary is a keen reader of this tale while, with an even clearer illustration of the hopelessly vicarious nature of their appeal, Madame Aubain in his *conte*, *Un Coeur simple* (1877) names her children Paul and Virginie, seemingly indifferent to the tragedy of the prototypes. This folly suggests that the work, short of actually impressing a sense of alterity on its readers, becomes a vogue adjusted rather too easily to the domestic bourgeois life of France. With his irony, Flaubert reopens the gap between text and life that Bernardin's novel tries to close.

*

Without some sense of the changes in the conception of self that it induces and the centrality of writing to the discussion, it is difficult to understand the nuances of eighteenth-century thought about travel. The debate between exoticism and universality makes way for a more agonised sense that the self is itself other. Moi in the *Neveu de Rameau* observes with a mixture of admiration and horror that Rameau is not himself. Someone else's nephew, a 'lui' relying on the perception of others rather than a 'moi' who exists in his own right, he is not an individual but endlessly dividual: 'Rien ne dissemble plus de lui que lui-même' (nothing differs more from himself than himself). It is in the same terms that Tourvel in *Les Liaisons dangereuses* tries to describe the complexity of the Valmontian mixture of love and malice in her troubled letter 161: 'Mais qu'il est différent de lui-même!' (but how different he is from himself!) Perhaps Valmont's very name (valley/mountain) contains the opposition in his character. Rousseau himself embodies this conflict most poignantly in constructing a dialogue between Jean-Jacques and Rousseau, *Rousseau juge de Jean-Jacques* (written in 1775-76). Here he constructs a dialogue between someone who has read Rousseau and someone who has met him and tries to reconcile their views. He epitomises the painful gap between the self as it experiences itself and as it is experienced in society and by others, or, as often, an intrinsic self and an authorial self. 'Il fallait nécessairement que je dise de quel oeil, si j'étais un autre, je verrais un homme tel que je suis' (it was absolutely necessary to say how, if I were another, I would view a man such as I am). It has been observed that Voltaire is at his happiest on the frontiers between town and country or between different lands, like Candide, Zadig and the Quaker where he can experience exile, alienation, disguise, pseudonyms as irritatingly necessary but as ultimately exhilarating. Diderot and Rousseau experience this dispossession with rather more anguish but take divergent routes in trying to come to terms with an authentic self. Rousseau abstracts the self in order to understand it. He tries to remove it from the pressures exerted by a duplicitous society. But Diderot's remark that 'il n'y a que le méchant qui soit seul' (only the evil person is alone) stings Rousseau. For Diderot the self, such as we can understand it, can only be virtuous in society because by virtue we really mean beneficence and beneficence requires the presence of the other. Travel takes many eighteenth-century writers on a journey of discovery to the vast continent of the self. The journey from self-affirmation to self-consciousness had been a short one.

Selected Reading

Michèle Duchet, *Anthropologie et histoire au siècle des 'Lumières'* (Paris: Albin Michel, 1995). In French. A study of alterity, with emphasis on colonialism, slavery and racism in the period.

Dena Goodman, *Criticism in Action: Enlightenment Experiments in Political Writing* London; Ithaca: Cornell University Press, 1989). A book which contains chapters on the dialogue between different cultures in *Lettres persanes*, the *Supplément au voyage de Bougainville* and Rousseau's second discourse.

Nicole Hafid-Martin, *Voyage et connaissance au tournant des Lumières (1780-1820)* (Oxford: Voltaire Foundation, 1995). In French. Contains a useful chapter on *Paul et Virginie*.

Charles Taylor, *Sources of the Self: The Making of the Modern Identity* (Cambridge: Cambridge University Press, 1994). An exhaustive study of the emergence of the self which includes a chapter entitled 'Radical Enlightenment'.

VII
Women

1. Defining Woman

Travel takes authors and thinkers on actual and imaginative journeys that guide them to new conclusions about human experience, as well as difficulties concerning language and text. But for many of these intrepid male explorers, there remains nothing stranger than woman. Women remain one of the great enigmas for the all-conquering philosophical writers of the eighteenth century. But they have their reasons for keeping it like this.

Descartes had argued for the primacy of the spirit as a realm distinct from the material space of extension. Mind precedes body, irrespective of the sex. This Cartesian affirmation of the autonomy of the mind was beneficial particularly to women who were more likely to be accused of being subject to their bodies. Poulain de la Barre's *De l'égalité des deux sexes*, published in 1673, was inspired by this revelation. Accordingly, there was a widespread if not universal admiration of the 'femme de lettres' (woman of letters). The 'femme savante' (woman of intellect) was no longer a subject chiefly fit for comedy. Women begin to embody the potential for the wider diffusion of learning. Madame d'Epinay, the Marquise du Châtelet and their like command more respect than surprise in philosophical circles. However, even those men most supportive of the education and reading of women seem to have reservations about an inherent instability in the character of women and educational opportunities for women were unquestionably inferior, despite the efforts of writers such as Laclos and Madame d'Epinay who takes on Rousseau's model of female education in her *Conversations d'Emilie* (1775).

Once again definitions of woman are bound with problems of

authorship and reading. When woman's moral character or the threats to it are discussed, reading seems often to be a root cause. Paintings depict the licence of women in different ways and, although gambling or drinking were vices among many women, images of the danger of reading are particularly common. Perhaps the attraction is the ambivalence of reading, for, unlike gambling and drinking, what is considered perilous is also considered to be salutary in many ways. Learning and licence are different sides of the same coin.

Habits of reading change in the course of the century. Books are increasingly consigned to a more private space where they are no longer read aloud. Eighteenth-century portraits prefer little books held by female hands to big volumes adorning the backdrop. Chardin, whose philosopher is seated before a lovely large folio, suggests that reading is an occasion to be marked by a corresponding formality in dress. It is still an honour and a privilege, but reading will now become a quiet communion between two subjectivities. Daniel Huet's preface to Madame de Lafayette's novel, *Zayde* (1670) was influential in arguing that the novel was a successful genre in France since, there in particular, women and men enjoyed a proximity propitious to such writing. The hegemony of women in France affords western society, and French culture in particular, its superiority over Eastern cultures. Voltaire echoes Huet in arguing that in the absence of women the arts could not flourish, hence the moribund state of culture in the Orient which they see. But just as such a climate favours the novel, so it jeopardises the likelihood of a good epic, the epitome of dignified and grand writing, coming to fruition. Madame Dacier, the translator of Homer's *Iliad* and the *Odyssey* in the early part of the eighteenth century, agreed that the failure of France to produce an epic must be ascribed to the obsessive national hobby of love and gallantry.

The female influence on men is widely, perhaps unanimously recognised, but opinions diverge as to whether this influence is healthy. Montesquieu writes that 'nous sommes tous femmes par esprit' (we all have the minds of women). This could be a statement celebrating the salutary wit and grace which characterise the intellectual life of the eighteenth century, but it is more likely, at least among serious thinkers, that there is something pejorative about Montesquieu's statement. There was an increasing backlash against the 'mollesse' (or softness) induced by the hegemony of women and the inordinate influence they enjoyed. In the *Lettres persanes* Usbek's harem is depicted as a cruelly unnatural environment, but he and Rica are also allowed to make quite telling observations about the excessive freedoms and influences enjoyed by women in France.

While woman is acknowledged to be the custodian of the arts, feminine sensitivity to their charms is considered to render her vulnerable to the wrong sort of novels. Jean-Baptiste Greuze's portrait of 1758/59 shows the dangers of reading for women. The young lady is reading Charles-Pierre Colardeau's *Lettres d'Héloïse à Abelard*, a French translation of Pope's *Eloisa to Abelard*. Inspired by her reading, she has fallen into reverie, seemingly oblivious to her semi-naked state and to the presence of the viewer. While the distraction in which Chardin's painting catches the philosopher is a sign of his gravitas, for the woman it denotes a neglect of her roles that is dangerous. Men are also susceptible to the power of reading but female rather than male readers are always feared since, it is acknowledged, their imaginations are more impressionable. In his *Essai sur le caractère, les moeurs et l'esprit des femmes dans les différents siècles*, published in 1772, Antoine Léonard Thomas marvels at the overwhelming power of the female imagination:

> On a observé que celle des femmes a je ne sais quoi de singulier et d'extraordinaire. Tout les frappe; tout se peint en elles avec vivacité [...] Le monde réel ne leur suffit pas; elles aiment à se créer un monde imaginaire; elles l'habitent et l'embellissent.

> (It has been observed that that of women has something mysteriously singular and extraordinary. Everything strikes them. To them everything is painted vividly [...] The real world is not enough for them; they enjoy creating an imaginary world; they inhabit and embellish it.)

However, given that so many women are already versed in

novels, just as man is irrevocably fallen in society, the novel itself is the only available remedy. Rousseau later argues, in *La nouvelle Héloïse*, his own rewriting of the story, that the novel can induce uplifting thoughts among women already given to lubricious reveries. It is in part by depicting a specific type of woman that Rousseau hopes to write a novel that will not lead women astray. This woman is the virtuous mother.

Greuze's *La Mère bien aimée* dates from 1769, ten years after the portrait. It contributes to the new iconography of the mother which owes much to Rousseau's *Julie* and *Emile*, published, in 1761 and 1762, between the two paintings. In Book one of *Emile* he argues that wet-nurses should be dispensed with so that women will stay at home. It looks as though it could be the same woman tempted to perilous thoughts who is now in the bosom of her family. It is an amazing depiction of her procreative potential. The mother's explicit role is to bear and rear children at home, under the proud gaze of her husband. The central role in the family as in the state remains that of the husband. These oppositions find expression in *Julie* where the heroine tries to reconcile the duties of motherhood and the demands of passion. This text becomes one of the most popular books of the century and changes the way people read. Reading is henceforward an intimate activity in which the subjectivity of reader and author are engaged. But while *Julie* is the incarnation of conflicting passion and maternal virtue, the distrust of woman's place in society grew. Sophie, Emile's mate, embodies values which teach women pre-eminently to be the companions of men, and the distrust of Rousseau is accompanied by the more aggressively masculine thought of the d'Holbach coterie later in the century.

Many works of the eighteenth century discuss women and their role in society. Of these a good number bring into play, whether self-consciously or not, the difficulties which result when men write about women, acknowledging that narratives about women remain male-oriented. Just as narratives about nature and authenticity remain by definition social and artificial, so the view of women is dictated by men. It is these works that will first be considered before works written by women are discussed.

L'abbé Prévost, Manon Lescaut *(1731)*

The *Histoire du chevalier Des Grieux et de Manon Lescaut* was published in the final volume of the *Mémoires d'un homme de qualité* in
1731 but is more commonly known as *Manon Lescaut*. Unlike *Paul
et Virginie*, where the harmony of nature is matched by that of the
sexes borne out by the title, any sense of proportion and balance
is unsettled from the start. While the text is about Manon Lescaut,
the woman who bears that name is no longer there. Likewise, while
the chevalier Des Grieux is the narrator of his story, we cannot
escape the impression that he is also a passive character in it. Des
Grieux tells the story of how, supplied with all the right aristocratic
credentials, he meets Manon and, smitten with love for her, is
deflected from the path of conventional respectability. After
numerous misadventures they flee to America where, finally, she
dies in the desert. Once again the attempt to find a new world and
to escape the conventions endowed by tradition is doomed. Once
Manon dies, Des Grieux returns to his *ancien régime* world where he
is welcomed back by his male friends and family. The denomina-
tion of natural spaces and phenomena and the presence of
inscriptions everywhere in *Paul et Virginie* intimate optimistically
that the text is not tainted irremediably by the society that has produced it. But here the intractable presence of a civilised narrative
does not allow us near to truths about nature or emotion. Where
Paul et Virginie uses the novel to compensate for truth when society
has broken down, *Manon Lescaut* sacrifices truth, one suspects, to
the dictate of social reconciliation.

Manon Lescaut shows firstly how the narrative can be used by a
man to justify himself and, secondly, how he can exploit the traditionally enigmatic qualities of a woman to justify himself to other
men and thereby integrate himself into society.

The narrative is a product of society rather than an ally of
nature and is therefore no innocent vehicle for the truth. For a
start, Des Grieux's narrative is bought. The 'homme de qualité'
who comes across Des Grieux and instantly recognises a man of
class, pays him to tell his story. The narrative, therefore, is itself created by the very mores it describes, and credibility is linked to
credit. The narrator is instinctively sympathetic to Des Grieux and

indeed, seemingly absorbed totally by his narrative, he does not resurface at the end as one might expect. Instead we are left with a missing bracket.

If the narrator appears to be won over by this discourse, Prévost brilliantly ensures that the version of events in the narrative appears to condemn Des Grieux even as it tries to justify him, thanks to a number of little hints and gaps. The language of Des Grieux's narrative obtrudes and reprocesses. Des Grieux's honesty about lying creates problems of interpretation for us. We are soon aware of the work his language has to do in trying to relate or as often compensate for actions that are, fundamentally, unaccountable. He maintains that 'Le désordre de mon âme... ne saurait être exprimé' (the disorder of my soul could not be expressed) or, when reading Manon's letter, he describes it as 'une des situations uniques auxquelles on n'a rien eprouvé qui soit semblable. On ne saurait les expliquer aux autres, parce qu'ils n'en ont pas l'idée' (one of those unique situations the like of which no-one has ever felt. They cannot be explained to the others because they do not have an idea of it). Curiously, he gets the best of both worlds in both pleading his uniqueness and appealing to our recognition of his predicament. His superlatives convey a phenomenon unintelligible to us, because untranslatable by language, while the plural ('une de ces situations') flatters us at the same time that it might nonetheless be comprehensible. The reader will be struck by the proliferation of conditionals and subjunctives, in addition to the conjunctions 'quoique' and 'malgré', in his narrative. Embedded beneath the folds of these subjunctives lies an implicit awareness of a clearer vision of reality that they struggle to repress: 'Quoique je conservasse tout le respect dû à l'autorité paternelle, l'âge et l'expérience avaient diminué beaucoup ma timidité' (although I conserved all the respect due to paternal authority, age and experience had dimished significantly all my timidity). We may reread this syntax as an admission that he does not conserve respect, but knows that he ought to do so. The characteristic 'quoique' is a key to the disjunction between the desired and the real version, a refuge for Des Grieux to reassure us of a coherent version when the evidence of the action seems to suggest otherwise. The exculpations and the attempts to accredit his narrative are laid on so thick that we are faced by the paradox that artful sophistication is enlisted somehow to explain his natural simplicity.

Although practically everyone else dies, sometimes as a result of his action, Des Grieux ensures that he dies repeatedly, but only in language: 'J'aurais donné mille vies pour être à son côté' (I would have given a thousand lives to be at her side) or 'Je me serais donné mille fois la mort, si je n'eusse pas eu dans mes bras le seul bien qui m'attachait à la vie' (I would have killed myself a thousand times if I had not the only possession which kept me alive in my arms) or 'je souffris mortellement sans Manon' (I suffered mortally without Manon, book one) or 'j'aime mieux mourir mille fois que d'avoir le moindre commerce désormais avec toi' (I prefer to die a thousand times over than to have the slightest truck with you from now on, book two). Not only does he fail to die even once, but he takes life. Des Grieux's language does not so much recapitulate as reprocess.

Narrative is then an aristocratic male prerogative that allows him to perpetuate his values while consigning woman to the role of character. Des Grieux's vocabulary stages an interplay of metaphorical and literal truths and terms that move between class and morality so that, for instance, 'noble' sentiments are doubly good. This tactic recalls the way natural reactions coincide with, or are indebted to, class-conditioned judgments in Marivaux's plays. Nietzsche, in the *Genealogy of Morals*, later will outline how our evaluation of morals and the terms in which we describe them have their roots in class distinctions. Des Grieux tries to relocate his nobility within the new codes of sensibility rather than hanging it on the traditional referents of birth and class. Wanting to be judged by his intentions rather than his actions, by an essential and transparent integrity, Des Grieux lays claim to what has been called an 'aristocracy of the soul'. And he claims for himself a superior sensibility. Good people are not those whose actions are 'good', but those who approve of him, who have an inner affinity with him. However, he has trouble in maintaining that his nobility is predicated on sublime feelings when the woman who elicits these feelings, Manon, is to all intents and purposes a prostitute.

Manon throws his values into confusion, for even the eloquent Des Grieux has difficulty in requiring her to be at once the chaste and virtuous consort worthy of his love, and the harlot responsible for leading him astray. Manon on one occasion forces him to look at himself in a mirror so that he cannot transfer onto her his contradictions. But he now rewrites Manon rather than reforming himself. A woman is an object more susceptible to this sort of activity, because it suits an overwhelmingly patriarchal society to view woman as strange. As Des Grieux marvels, 'Manon était une créature d'un caractère extraordinaire' (Manon was a creature of extraordinary character). The fact that he has murdered someone and committed other atrocities can be forgiven or better still forgotten in the face of the greater curiosity of a woman's conduct. This can be compared with the familiarly awestruck terms in which Thomas describes the female imagination ('ceile des femmes a je ne sais quoi de singulier et d'extraordinaire') or with Diderot's exclamation in his short essay *Sur les femmes*: 'O femmes! vous êtes des enfants bien extraordinaires!' (O women! you are quite extraordinary children). These outbursts recall Trivelin's assessment of Silvia's defiant love for Arlequin in Marivaux's *La Double inconstance* (1723):

Mon sentiment à moi est qu'il y a quelque chose d'extraordinaire dans cette fille-là. Refuser ce qu'elle refuse, cela n'est point naturel, ce n'est point là une femme, voyez-vous, c'est quelque créature d'une espèce à nous inconnue.

(My feeling if you ask me is that there is something extraordinary in that girl there. Refusing what she refuses, that is not natural, that's not the behaviour of a woman, don't you see, but that of some creature belonging to a species unknown to us.)

Trivelin refuses to countenance this behaviour as that of a woman, such is the narrow definition circumscribing a woman's character and conduct. Recourse to this same hyperbole allows us to marvel at the oddity of Silvia's behaviour rather than the injustice of the convention to which she will not bend. Even Figaro, momentarily suspicious of Suzanne in Beaumarchais's *Le Mariage de Figaro*, lapses into this pseudo-physiological vocabulary to express the inexpressibly deviant behaviour of woman. Although he listened sympathetically to his mother's feminist tirade, the distressed Figaro quickly lapses into viewing woman, in the same way as Trivelin, as unnatural and yet also a creature subject to instinct rather than reason:

> O femme, femme, femme! créature faible et décevante! ... nul animal créé ne peut manquer à son instinct; le tien est donc de tromper?

> (Oh woman, woman, woman! You feeble and disappointing creature! ... no animal in God's creation can avoid his instinct; yours is then to deceive?)

This dynamic is visible in *Les Liaisons dangereuses.* Rather than condemning Merteuil's conduct in absolute terms of right and wrong, again it is considered even by the benevolent Madame de Rosemonde to be particularly unworthy of a woman: 'on rougit d'être femme, quand on en voit une capable de tels excès' (you blush to be a woman, when you see one of them capable of such excesses). Even though she is, of course, closely related to Valmont, this female kinship troubles her beyond any others. A woman is once again not considered as an individual but as the representative of a species that confounds men. Moreover, it is clear that while society has the mechanisms for dealing with and rehabilitating deviant men, women cannot be reaccommodated. This is spelt out most clearly by the contrast between the emotion (letter 165) elicited by Valmont's death which is commemorated by an affirmative and restorative vocabulary of honour and courage and the consternation that meets Merteuil's exile. The contrast is made more explicit by the resurgence in the final letters of Prévan, the playboy outsmarted by Merteuil in an earlier episode, whose acts are now forgiven and fêted.

Like Manon, Merteuil is expelled from society. While Manon is denied a voice and indeed a life, the army or the knights of Malta or the duel are there for Des Grieux as they are for other men who fall foul of society. They offer a sort of safety net paradoxically because of the honourable dangers which men run there. Roxane's suicide at the end of the *Lettres persanes* puts to shame

Usbek's high-minded flight to France and, notwithstanding the possible ironies there, represents a grasp over her own life even as she ends it. Likewise torn between natural and cultural definitions of woman, Julie and Virginie die. But the condemnation of Merteuil is perhaps the most savage, since she is denied the transcendence of death and the honour or relief it brings.

3. Women Writing

It is above all the compulsion to write that undoes Merteuil, for as Paul Valéry says, 'écrire, c'est avoir besoin des autres' (writing means needing others), and she cannot enjoy absolute independence when writing. Language is both necessary to her independence and fatal to it. Her chief mistake is to think that her vaunted vision can be translated with impunity into language. Cécile's naïveté is made clear by her promise in the first line of the first letter to 'tenir parole' or 'to keep her word'. Merteuil resolves not to undergo the fate of Manon and feature merely as a character in someone else's discourse. A number of women try to become the authors of a destiny that others will otherwise write for them. It is through their mastery of language that women, like some men of the lower orders, can hope to accede to the power otherwise denied them. The exchange of letters in *Les Liaisons dangereuses* produces an equality subversive of the power structures foreseen by society. Men and women become writers equally adept at using language to hide the truth. Vice and the freedom from rules it entails, seems to produce a level playing field that virtue, at least as defined by society, does not permit, since, as Merteuil comments, winning for women means not losing. Rosine, in *Le Mariage de Figaro*, observes in a similar vein that her victory consists in retaining a man rather than trying to win one. In the first letters Cécile quotes her mother insistently, prefiguring a fate where her discourse and life will be dictated by others.

Merteuil explains in her letter 81 that she has achieved complete autonomy and that, in learning to read and observe, she has become the author of her own destiny rather than a character in it. She decides 'je puis dire que je suis mon ouvrage' (I can say that I am my own work). Of course in writing this to Valmont she is endangering the autonomy she is celebrating. All works need a reader and, as the authors of eighteenth-century works painfully realise, this is a reader whose reactions and respect cannot be relied upon. Not only does Merteuil master the nuances of her own language, but she sets about appropriating that of others, but she is finally trapped by the letters that she has written, and Valmont, whose memoirs she magnanimously proposed to write, kindly disseminates the letters of this woman writer. Laclos seals Merteuil's fate with bitter irony, for the metaphors she manipulates seem to become literalised and her words turn against her. All her assertions of superior vision, like that in the first letter, 'vous voyez, l'amour ne m'aveugle pas' (you see, love is not blinding me), ironically prefigure her loss of an eye and, with it, her loss of face.

Like Merteuil, a good number of women resolve to create through writing a positive and autonomous identity for themselves and for woman. Reading was in many cases controversial enough for women. When women turn to writing this is naturally considered to be presumptuous and dangerous. But numerous women wrote and had their works published. Perhaps the most spectacular success was the *Lettres d'une Péruvienne* by Madame de Graffigny, published first in 1747 and subsequently in over one hundred editions and translations.

Madame de Graffigny [or Grafigny], Lettres d'une Péruvienne *(1747)*

Françoise de Graffigny was born in 1695 and, after marrying in 1712, became the victim of physical abuse by her husband. She obtained a legal separation and began a career in writing. With a versatility characteristic of the Enlightenment she wrote plays, children's stories and fables, but it was the *Lettres d'une Péruvienne* that won most attention. The letters are those of a Peruvian princess Zilia who is removed by kidnapping forces from her homeland and her prospective husband, Aza. She learns to write both in order to comment on the strange society she enters and to express her love and yearning for Aza. The text typifies the enlightenment in trying to unite a satire of the immediate social circumstances of the day and a celebration of sensibility and love. In letter 34 she writes to Aza:

En général, il me semble que les femmes naissent ici, bien plus com-
munément que chez nous, avec toutes les dispositions nécessaires
pour égaler les hommes en mérite et vertus. Mais, comme s'ils en
convenaient au fond de leur coeur, et que leur orgueil ne pût sup-
porter cette égalité, ils contribuent en toute manière à les rendre
méprisables, soit en manquant de considération pour les leurs, soit
en séduisant celle des autres [...] Et en effet, mon cher Aza, comment ne seraient-elles pas révoltées contre l'injustice des loix qui
tolèrent l'impunité des hommes, poussée au même excès que leur
autorité? [...] Il est autorisé à punir rigoureusement l'apparence
d'une légère infidélité, en se livrant sans honte à toutes celles que
le libertinage lui suggère. Enfin, mon cher Aza, il semble qu'en
France les liens du mariage ne soient réciproques qu'au moment de
la célébration et que dans la suite, les femmes seules y doivent être
assujetties.

(In general it seems to me that women here are born much more
frequently than in our homeland with all the attributes necessary to
equal men in merit and virtue. Seemingly conceding this equality in
the bottom of their hearts but unable to tolerate it on account of
their pride, men here do all they can to make women contemptible
by either showing a lack of respect for their own wives or seducing
those of others [...] And indeed, dearest Aza, how could these
women not be revolted by the injustice of laws that tolerate men's
impunity, which is pushed to the same extreme as their authority?
[...] He is authorised to punish harshly the appearance of a slight
infidelity while abandoning himself shamelessly to all those that libertinage suggests to him. In the end, dearest Aza, it seems that in
France the bonds of marriage are reciprocal only at the moment the
wedding is celebrated and that thereafter only wives must be subject
to them.)

Zilia's satirical observations are weighed against an implicit
norm of mutual respect and decency which is the basis of the
loving relationship she enjoys with Aza to whom she writes these
letters. It is therefore a cruel blow when the beloved Aza, for whom
she has waited and yearned for so long, finally appears, only to
abandon her for a new Spanish woman he has decided to marry.

Even he has been corrupted by Spain where he was exiled. The satire levelled at French society's treatment of women becomes cruelly universalised. This betrayal seems to suggest a tragically fundamental distance between the sexes. Man and woman seem ultimately as remote from one another as Aza and Zilia, as A and Z.

Zilia's letters not only direct the attention of Aza and the reader to a set of observations about contemporary French society, but exemplify how a woman may benefit, intellectually and spiritually, from writing. She is particularly scathing about the education of French women and enthusiastic about the potential that reading offers women. The letters are initially a means of trying to commune with Aza, and she uses a supply of *quipus* (a Peruvian system of knots) that she has brought with her to write to him. As they start to run out the economy with which she must use them and the need to learn French is emphasised. But, already before Aza abandons her, it becomes clear that writing becomes an act of pleasure, a benefit and a salvation, whether or not it is committed to commerce with a particular reader. Her correspondence with Aza is, she admits to herself in letter 18, the pretext for an understanding of her own feelings and doubts:

Combien de temps effacé de ma vie, mon cher Aza! Le soleil a fait la moitié de son cours depuis la dernière fois que j'ai joui du bonheur artificiel que je me faisais en croyant m'entretenir avec toi. Que cette double absence m'a paru longue! [...] A peine puis-je encore former ces figures, que je me hâte d'en faire les interprètes de ma tendresse. Je me sens ranimer par cette tendre occupation. Rendue à moi-même, je crois recommencer à vivre. Aza, que tu m'es cher, que j'ai de joie à te le dire, à le peindre, à donner ce sentiment toutes les sortes d'existences qu'il peut avoir!

(How much time has been erased from my life! The Sun has made half its journey, dearest Aza, since the last time I enjoyed the artificial pleasure I created for myself by believing that I was conversing with you. How long this double absence has seemed to me! [...] I am still barely able to form these figures that I rush to make the interpreters of my tenderness. I feel myself being brought back to life by this tender occupation. Restored to myself, I feel as if I am beginning to live again. Oh Aza, how dear you are to me, what joy I feel in telling you so, in depicting this fact, in giving this sentiment all the kinds of existence it can have!)

It is sufficient to imagine, rather than necessary to have, a reader. As compelling as the need to declare to Aza her love for him is the attraction of writing itself. She writes as much of the pleasure of writing as the pleasure she associates with him. Discovering that a 'bonheur artificiel' can restore her to herself, Zilia anticipates the values Rousseau finds in writing, for his heroine Julie takes a similar pleasure in writing letters. Graffigny also explores the way writing expresses and supports love and virtue, yoking these feelings to solitude innovatively. Even as Zilia gives joyous expression to her love, she indicates a degree of autonomy and a taste for solitude afforded and enhanced by the pen.

Zilia is fortunate to profit from the kindness of a French friend and admirer of hers by the name of Déterville (who shows that men and women seem reconcilable in friendship after all) to become a truly autonomous woman. Although she has been rebuffed by Aza, she refuses to marry Déterville at the end of the novel, thereby protecting her independence. Her final letters, now addressed to Déterville, suggest more optimistically that they will, nevertheless, remain great friends and that friendship is sustainable, even across the boundaries of sexuality, culture and nationality. She becomes, before Rousseau appears, an elegant advocate of solitude:

Vous craignez en vain que la solitude n'altère ma santé. Croyez-moi, Déterville, elle ne devient jamais dangereuse que par l'oisiveté [...] Le plaisir d'être; ce plaisir oublié, ignoré même de tant d'aveugles humains; cette pensée si douce, ce bonheur si pur, je suis, je vis, j'existe, pourrait seul rendre heureux, si l'on en jouissait. Si l'on en connaissait le prix.

(You fear needlessly that solitude might damage my health. Believe me, Déterville, solitude never becomes dangerous save on account of idleness [...] The pleasure of being – a forgotten pleasure not even known to so many blind humans – that thought so sweet, that happiness so pure, 'I am, I live, I exist' could bring happiness all by itself if one remembered it, if one enjoyed it, if one treasures it as befits its worth.)

The writing of Zilia and Madame de Graffigny not only points out the shortcomings of a society unfavourable to women but shows how through words the sentiments, the autonomy, in short the life of an individual may be restored to its full potential.

If, as Zilia observes in her letters, the opportunities to write were limited, women presided over the *salons* and exercised great influence over the direction and form that the writings of men took. The eighteenth century is the golden age of the *salons*, the regular assemblies organised by women for the purposes of discussing intellectual ideas. The most famous *salons* were presided over by Madame Geoffrin, Madame du Deffand, Mademoiselle de Lespinasse and Madame Necker. In the latter years of the century many thinkers reacted against the influence of women and tried to affirm more serious, masculine models, whether in political or aesthetic terms. The 'mollesse' (softness) which Voltaire celebrated in *Le Mondain* was now unacceptable. Diderot was not alone in rejecting the gallantry of genre painting in favour of a more robust moral tonality, while Rousseau objected most vigorously to the femininisation of society which was anathema to his Republican conception of the state and maintained that women's virtue could only be properly exercised within the home.

Indeed, when the Revolution swept in Republican ideas, women found that they were more than ever seen as a threat to sobriety, reason, justice and lucidity and that they would not benefit as women from the *Déclaration des droits de l'homme et du citoyen* (declaration of the rights of man and the citizen) adopted by the *Assemblée nationale* in 1789. Two years later, and two years before she was executed, Olympe de Gouges, born Marie Gouze (1748-93), the prolific author of plays and pamphlets committed in equal measure to fiction and to polemical argument, wrote a *Déclaration des droits de la femme et de la citoyenne* which, largely ignored then, remains a powerful indictment both of the culpability of the Revolutionaries and the fallibility of woman.

Olympe de Gouges, Déclaration des droits de la femme et de la citoyenne *(1791)*

Olympe de Gouges begins her work by imploring 'le sexe supérieur en beauté comme en courage dans les souffrances maternelles' (the sex of superior beauty and of courage in maternal suffering) to recognise and press for her right to benefit from the new liberties. In a 'postambule' (or postface) to a number of articles she drafts in order to supplement the rights of man, Gouges departs from the careful, legal language of the articles to an impassioned tone:

Femme, réveille-toi; le tocsin de la raison se fait entendre dans tout l'univers; reconnaîs tes droits. Le puissant empire de la Nature n'est plus environné de préjugés, de fanatisme, de superstition et de mensonges. Le flambeau de la vérité a dissipé tous les nuages de la sottise et de l'usurpation. L'homme esclave a multiplié ses forces, a eu besoin de recourir aux tiennes pour briser ses fers. Devenu libre, il est devenu injuste envers sa compagne. Ô femmes! Femmes, quand cesserez-vous d'être aveugles? Quels sont les avantages que vous avez recueillis dans la révolution? Un mépris plus marqué, un dédain plus signalé. Dans les siècles de corruption vous n'avez régné que sur la faiblesse des hommes. Votre empire est détruit.

(Woman, wake up; the tocsin of reason can be heard across the whole universe; recognise your rights. The powerful empire of Nature is no longer surrounded by prejudices, fanaticism, superstition and lies. The torch of truth has dissipated all the clouds of foolishness and usurpation. Slavish man has multiplied his forces and needed to resort to yours to break his fetters. Now free, he has become unjust to his female companion. O women! Women, when will you cease to be blind? What advantages have you gained from the Revolution? Only more pronounced contempt, more overt disdain. In the centuries of corruption you reigned only over the weakness of men. Your empire has been destroyed.)

Olympe de Gouges heralds the arrival of reason (as Voltaire had earlier when announcing Newton) in terms which are not soberly rational. She at first implores woman to hear and then to see. This assault mounted on the different senses assists the hyperbolic, or highly exaggerated, observation that reason has taken hold in 'tout l'univers' and renders inexcusable the passivity that Gouges sees as characteristic of women. She moves from the singular ('Femme, réveille-toi') to a plural ('Ô femmes!') in a great crescendo of anger. This anger is inflamed by her realisation that the Revolution has not only failed to help woman as might have been expected, but that its reforms have cost her dearly. In a chiasmus (a literary figure where the word order is mirrored) she laments the fortunes of 'ce sexe autrefois méprisable et respecté, et depuis la révolution, respectable et méprisé' (this sex once detestable and respected and, since the revolution, respectable and detested).

Like Rousseau, Gouges looks back to earlier times vilified by the Enlightenment in order to argue that their shortcomings were more liberating than the virtues which have replaced them. Just as Rousseau hoped and believed that evil could contain its own remedy, so Gouges observes that 'Sous l'Ancien Régime, tout était vicieux, tout était coupable; mais ne pourrait-on pas apercevoir l'amélioration des choses dans la substance même des vices?' (under the ancien Régime, all was evil, all was guilt-ridden; but could you not see things getting better in the very substance of vices?). Gouges's view that good and evil are not polar opposites but subsets or byproducts of one another is characteristic of the Enlightenment's discovery that the enemy may lie within its own camp.

Although the century was punctuated by frustrated attempts to improve the unacceptably inferior status of women, Gouges looks back during the Revolution at a female Empire which has declined since then. The new Republic favoured a new more masculine model of virtue, while the Republic of letters received a new constitution too. The *salons* were one of its casualties, as the Revolution instituted all-male clubs and societies. The last word of the Revolution's glorious triad, Liberté, égalité and fraternité, would have the last word on *salon* culture.

Selected Reading

Roland Bonnel and Catherine Rubinger (eds), *Femmes savantes et femmes d'esprit: Women intellectuals of the French Eighteenth Century* (New York: Peter Lang, 1994). A study primarily of philosophical and scientific women.

Dena Goodman, *The Republic of Letters: A Cultural History of the French Enlightenment* (London: Ithaca: Cornell University Press, 1994). An authoritative study of the way society and the canon in the nineteenth century marginalised the works of eighteenth-century woman, with many interesting insights into *salon* culture.

Katharine A. Jensen, *Writing Love: Letters, Women, and the Novel (1605-1776)* (Carbondale: Southern Illinois UP, 1994). A work which discusses Madame de Graffigny in detail.

Sara E. Melzer and Leslie Rabine, eds, *Rebel Daughters: Women and the French Revolution* (Oxford: Oxford University Press, 1992). A work which contains a chapter on Olympe de Gouges's rights for women.

Dorinda Outram, *The Body and the French Revolution: Sex, Class and Political Culture* (New Haven: Yale University Press, 1989).

Naomi Segal, *The Unintended Reader: Feminism and* Manon Lescaut (Cambridge: Cambridge University Press, 1986). A sophisticated feminist reading of *Manon Lescaut*.

Samia Spencer (ed.), *French Women and the Age of Enlightenment* (Bloomington: Indiana University Press, 1985). A series of essays which covers different aspects of women's activities in the Enlightenment.

VIII

Theatre

In *Les Liaisons dangereuses*, the Marquise de Merteuil is unmasked and humiliated in a theatre. This is possibly ironic given her wish to stage and direct others in her plots, but also characteristic in that the theatre is throughout the eighteenth century an important social space where standards of morality were overseen. Not only did the theatre attract audiences from the full range of social strata, but these audiences were themselves integral to the experience of the theatre as they no longer are. If only because of the lighting and design of the stage shared by audience and actors, the theatre seemed to be as often watched and judged in eighteenth-century theatres. These constraints, allied to the tendency of eighteenth-century thinkers to view æsthetic and social phenomena as interdependent realms, ensured that the theatre is a privileged locus of discussions which not only centre on the merits of particular plays, but instance many of the social and philosophical problems which tease thinkers elsewhere. Through its social stature and physical nature, the theatre attracts wider arguments concerning the merits of representation, the tensions between sincerity and duplicity, reason and emotion, self and other.

Theories of theatre tend to be the work of practitioners as well as theorists. As eighteenth-century philosophy looks to life, dramatic theory requires the experience of the stage to check its abstraction. These theories were themselves shaped by new influences rather than old precedents. Shakespeare exerted a new influence in France and helped towards the wider authorisation of subjects drawn from more recent history rather than Classical sources. Much as French playwrights clung to the unities of time, place and action (as laid down by Aristotle), as well as other conventions that underpinned Classical tragedy, the theatre increasingly could not be isolated from the fashions and beliefs of the age. Indeed, on the contrary, it began to be seen to shape these movements. By dedicating his tragedy *Zaïre* (1732) to Sir Everard Fawkener, a mere merchant from England, Voltaire announces shamelessly, in fact proudly, that commerce is a new avenue for patronage but also that its practices and values are worthy of the theatre.

Increasingly, it was felt that tragedy, at which the previous century had excelled, was inadmissible in an age less pessimistic about the human condition, but more pessimistic about its own talents. Upheavals in the sensibilities of the age could not be represented and satisfied only by reforms within tragedy. Indeed, the *foyers* of reform and renewal lay largely outside tragedy; the *Théâtre italien* (or the *Comédie-italienne*), which had been banned in 1697, was reintroduced in 1716 before merging with the *Opéra-Comique* (opera with spoken recitatives) in 1762. The *Théâtres de la foire* were entertainments performed at the fairs in Paris (the Foire Saint-Germain in winter and the Foire Saint-Martin in summer). Comedy is perhaps the form *par excellence* in which eighteenth-century playwrights find their voice. But slowly comedy was supplanted by a new, serious, moral form of drama, known indeed as the 'genre sérieux' (serious genre). Also known as the *drame* or the *drame bourgeois*, like its German cousin, the *bürgerliches Trauerspiel*, these plays, which aimed to mix comedy and tragedy, depicted the lives of ordinary people and rehabilitated the bourgeois as a subject fit for the stage. The validation of a bourgeois morality in plays was accompanied by a revision of the conventional assumptions about those who acted in them. Actors had yet to shake off the suspicion that they were prostituting themselves in public, and they were yet denied the right to Christian burial. Eighteenth-century writers predictably take up arms against such prejudice, but in some cases continue to regard the vocation of the actor as intriguing, even disquieting.

1. The Actor and Society

In common with other writers, Voltaire makes it clear that some form of appreciation of the arts is the corollary to an understanding of the principles of justice. The actor should therefore be recognised as an agent instrumental to the performance and success of arts, a figure in short as worthy of the nation's honours as anyone else. Voltaire looks again to England to report that Anne Oldfield (1683-1730), one of its great actresses, was buried in Westminster Abbey alongside the most illustrious national figures. The church's condemnation of actors was deemed to be another flagrant instance of its corruption. In his poem on the death of the tragic actress, Adrienne Lecouvreur, who was not afforded a Christian burial (1731), Voltaire laments not only the death itself of the actress but the extinction of a nation unable to produce great art or appreciate those who bring it to us.

When David Garrick's death in 1779 'eclipsed the gaiety of the nations', Dr. Johnson was exaggerating but only somewhat. In one of these nations, France, the actor's influence in determining how a role should be interpreted became more pronounced. Perhaps because the playwright after the 'grand siècle' is perceived to lack the creative genius of his predecessors but is subordinate to and sometimes even humiliated by the prejudices of those to whom he must entrust his play, the actor seems to grow in stature and is increasingly liberated and validated as a more autonomous force. In the course of the eighteenth century, a continually changing emphasis in the ascendancy of playwright, patron, audience, censor and director rendered plays as vulnerable to the sort of tortuous processes which detached texts from the finished and mediated products, books.

Written for the *Italiens*, the troupe of Italian actors installed at the *Comédie-italienne*, Marivaux's plays exploit such a sense of estrangement of the actor from the role and examine what happens when foreigners speak French. This is not in order to laugh at silly foreigners (although Beaumarchais does get Guillaume to speak with a horrendous German accent in *La Mère coupable*) but because in some sense we are all foreigners to language and find, even when speaking our own language, that it can be strange to us. Diderot indeed went to the theatre with his ears blocked up to try to understand better what happens if you cannot hear, let alone understand, anything, and he is interested in the different language blind or mute people speak. The stage interests those troubled by the discrepancies between seeing and reading when writing about experience in the natural world.

Voltaire himself acted all his life. This constant staging of himself squares with and accounts for his aesthetic in all matters, while Rousseau's rejection of the theatre epitomises a desire for transparency also to be found in his entire oeuvre. Voltaire's interest in the theatre as a national trophy and his concern for its place within culture and the nation is contested by Rousseau, while Voltaire's fascination with the role assumed by the self in acting is elaborated by Diderot in his theoretical writings.

Rousseau, Lettre à d'Alembert sur les spectacles *(1758)*

When, entrusted with the *Encylopédie* entry for 'Genève', d'Alembert wrote that Geneva would benefit from having a theatre without which it could not count as a truly civilised place, Rousseau answers d'Alembert's article in a public letter known as the *Lettre à d'Alembert* (1758). Here he argues that, on the contrary, a theatre would damage the moral health of Geneva, which was still an independent Republic.

Critiques of the theatre were not new, though in general neo-Classical sensibilities had satisfied themselves that the decorum of the theatre refined taste and manners. While some parts of the Church had remained distrustful, the Jesuits defended the theatre as part of their Counter-Reformation onslaught. Rousseau's arguments are in part neo-Platonic and Puritan, but his thought on theatre is informed by his own ideas expressed elsewhere in his oeuvre. Rousseau makes clear that a Republic, whether Geneva or an idealised state, must preserve its identity by resisting cultural Imperialism. The cosmopolitan dimension to the theatre is precisely what damages it. In this he is once again taking on a dearly held Enlightenment conviction and showing it merely to be an assumption. The layout of the title page indicates the importance Geneva has to him and the pride he takes in his own lonely uniqueness.

J.-J. Rousseau
Citoyen de Genève

A M. D'Alembert,
De l'Académie française, de l'Académie Royale des Sciences de

Paris, de celle de Prusse, de la Société Royale de Londres, de l'Académie Royale des Belles-Lettres de Suède, et de l'Institut de Bologne

Rousseau seems very generous in recording the accolades that d'Alembert has received, but the contrast is designed to strengthen his self-image. Unstinting in detailing d'Alembert's *cv*, Rousseau suggests that his own citizenship is as extensive and definitive a qualification of merit. Rousseau derives enough inner satisfaction from this citizenship to be able to live without all these endorsements. But d'Alembert resembles an actor strutting the international stage and collecting applause wherever he goes. Rousseau proceeds to describe the actor in terms which recall those relating to the fragmented and unhappy 'homme sociable' (sociable man) in the *Second Discourse*:

> Qu'est-ce que le talent du comédien? L'art de se contrefaire, de revêtir un autre caractère autre que le sien, de paraître différent de ce qu'on est, de se passionner de sang froid, de dire autre chose que ce qu'on pense aussi naturellement que si l'on le pensait réellement, et d'oublier enfin sa propre place à force de prendre celle d'autrui.

> (What does the talent of the actor consist of? The art of disguising oneself, of taking on a character other than one's own, of appearing different from what one is, of working oneself coolly into a passion, of saying things at variance with what one thinks as naturally as though one really believed it, and finally of forgetting one's proper place in taking that of others.)

The actor then perniciously plays out roles for others, a flagrant example of the self that lives for others as other. Actors do not do themselves any good in forsaking themselves. Nor, as the title page suggests, do their efforts to impress everyone else do their nations any good. The implication is that Rousseau makes the better servant to his nation. The theatre corrupts a people who should be satisfied with national celebrations of unity. Rousseau proceeds to examine some plays in order to argue that they cannot, as they pretend, strengthen virtue. In a critique of Molière's *Le Misanthrope*, he argues that comedy is dangerous since its ridicule punishes not vice but unconformity. When Rousseau defends the misanthrope as an embodiment of virtue who should not be treated as a laughing stock, there is no doubt at least a little investment of his own story into the analysis.

Rousseau's opposition to d'Alembert's suggestion was itself, predictably, opposed in different quarters. By 1769, when he wrote the posthumously published *Paradoxe sur le comédien* (paradox on the actor), Diderot had, like everyone else, fallen out with Rousseau. Jean-Jacques's visit of him in Vincennes prison was now but a distant memory. Rousseau describes the actor as 'un mélange de bassesse, de fausseté, de ridicule orgueil, et d'indigne avilissement, qui le rend propre à toutes sortes de personnages, hors le plus noble de tous, celui d'homme qu'il abandonne' (a mixture of baseness, falsity, ridiculous pride and undignified abasement which makes him ideal for playing any number of characters, apart from the most noble of all, that of the man he leaves behind). There could hardly be a better description of Diderot's intriguing, compelling figure of the 'Neveu de Rameau', an outsider to himself, who is always stalked by the Other in himself. But in the *Paradoxe sur le comédien*, another dialogue (this time between two speakers unimaginatively called Premier and Second), Diderot contests in various ways Rousseau's arguments about the effects that acting may have on the self and society. Increasingly, Diderot invested in the 'drame bourgeois' or drama, believing that this sentimental genre had the optimal capacity to move and improve its audiences, but it is the ambivalence of the actor, this figure standing at the junction of the written and the oral, the rational and the physical, at the intersection of different symbolic systems, that interests Diderot above all in the *Paradoxe sur le comédien*.

Diderot, Paradoxe sur le comédien *(1769)*

Earlier in the century, thinkers and actors alike had entertained different, often opposing, views when considering the qualities required of a good actor. They could not agree in particular about the optimal distribution of sentiment and reason in the actor.

Diderot's text asks whether the self should surrender to its sensibility or privilege the organising, synthesising capacity of its reason. Diderot, typically, gives expression to both views in a dialogue that tries itself to balance reason and sentiment. However, as his name perhaps suggests, the interlocutor by the name of Premier tends to enjoy the ascendancy in this discussion. He argues that actors must not even approximately feel the sentiments they portray, but that their intellect must take on the appearance of such sentiments. He prescribes his ideal actor thus: 'il me faut dans cet homme un spectateur froid et tranquille; j'en exige, par conséquent, de la pénétration et nulle sensibilité' (for me this man must be a cold and calm spectator: I demand of him, as a result, a penetrative mind and no sensibility whatsoever). The Premier then seems to be validating the capacity to 'se passionner de sang froid' which Rousseau deplored in the *Lettre à d'Alembert*. So while spectators are subject to their feelings, actors become the true spectators, their own spectators:

> Nous sentons, nous; eux, ils observent, étudient et peignent. Le dirai-je? Pourquoi non? La sensibilité n'est guère la qualité d'un grand génie. Ce n'est pas son coeur, c'est sa tête qui fait tout.

> (We are the ones who feel; As for them, they observe, study and paint. Shall I say it? Why not? Sensibility is hardly the quality of a great genius. It's not his heart but his head that does everything.)

Good actors master their feelings and tame their sensibility so that, as Premier argues, older men are in fact better at playing young men than young men who remain more susceptible to passion. Premier's convictions are not only designed to reflect speculatively on the qualities required of a good actor. He also argues that in 'la comédie du monde' (the theatre of the world), a metaphor deployed recurrently to show how life outside the theatre is governed similarly to life inside it, both the prosperity of society and our success in it depend crucially on such a capacity to exercise rational command over ourselves. Both good actors and good citizens regulate their sensibility with reason. The useless, fragmented citizen that Rousseau sees reflected in and encour-

aged by the actor is, Premier argues, analogous only to the bad
actor, for good actors are equivalent to good citizens, while enthu-
siasts cannot contribute to society.

These observations, which are not answered satisfactorily by the
Second, constitute, it might seem, the archetypal Enlightenment
credo of which we have been in search. But this one is, like others,
subject to qualification, because the examples which illustrate the
power of the good actors also show their danger. The Premier's
belief in the supremacy of reason over sensibility rests in part on
the argument that reason can successfully pretend to be sensibility.
It can operate more passionately than passion. Thanks to a curiously alternative physiology, the good actor gets reason to act its
opposite:

> Les larmes du comédien descendent de son cerveau; celles de
> l'homme sensible montent de son coeur: ce sont les entrailles qui
> troublent sans mesure la tête de l'homme sensible; c'est la tête de
> comédien qui porte quelquefois un trouble passager dans ses
> entrailles; il pleure comme un prêtre incrédule qui prêche la
> Passion; comme un séducteur aux genoux d'une femme qu'il
> n'aime pas, mais qu'il veut tromper.

> (The tears of the actor come down from his brain; those of the sen-
> sitive man rise up from his heart: it is the entrails which disturb
> immeasurably the head of the sensitive man; it is the head of the
> actor which transmits sometimes a momentary trouble into his
> entrails; he weeps like a faithless priest who preaches about the
> Passion; like a seducer at the knees of a woman whom he does not
> love but wants to cheat.)

These examples of priests and seducers carry us out of the theatre onto the stage which is the wider world, an insincere society
where the ability to persuade and deceive are crucial components
of our survival kit. Good actors know not only how to win an audience over, but how to cheat their way through society. In ordering
the passions, reason teaches you to become a master not only of
acting but of deception.

We may recall d'Alembert's statement in the *Discours préliminaire* that pays tribute to the power but also the danger of eloquence which results from the marriage of passion and reason. When eloquence and passion are the advocates of reason anyone can be taken prisoner. Premier's examples of the connivance of reason and passion are foreshadowed and echoed in numerous works of the century. Des Grieux's orchestrated sensibilities in *Manon Lescaut* exemplify the persuasive power of this alliance earlier in the century while, later, *Les Liaisons dangereuses* stages two characters who are frighteningly adept at acting in society for their own interests. Valmont knows all the combinations of reason and passion to force his way into the most morally secure safes of society. The other embodiment of rational control in *Les Liaisons dangereuses*, Merteuil, relates that, in order to succeed in society, she came to the realisation that 'il suffisait de joindre à l'esprit de l'auteur, le talent d'un comédien [...] mais au lieu de rechercher les vains applaudissements du théâtre, je résolus d'employer à mon bonheur ce que tant d'autres sacrifiaient à la vanité' (it was enough to link to the wit of the author the talent of the actor [...] but instead of looking for the vain applause of the theatre, I resolved to dedicate to my happiness what so many others sacrificed to their vanity). Merteuil learns from the stage how to operate in society. And she teaches those complacently inclined to rejoice in the pre-eminence of reason that precisely because it is the supreme force, reason can not only subjugate its opposite but become it.

The theoretical discussions of the destiny of the self on the stage, and its implications for society, undertaken variously by Rousseau and Diderot, have already been enacted on the stage: Pierre Carlet Chamblain de Marivaux (1688-1763) did not instantly attract the attention of philosophical *milieux*. His plays, which borrow the characters from the *Commedia dell'arte*, the stylised Italian popular theatre introduced to France in the sixteenth century and put on at the *Comédie italienne*, may have seemed familiar and predictable, both in their formal construction and in the conclusions to which they led, but these comedies, now anchored firmly in the modern repertoire, anticipate with great subtlety many questions that would be asked later in the century.

2. Marivaux

If Rousseau will later try to show that an already vulnerable, elusively essential self is compromised further once it is represented on the stage, Marivaux's plays show that it is through the perceptions of others on the stage which is society that we define and understand ourselves, that in fact even our most intimate sense of self is administered through the opinions of others or, more precisely, through what we think others think of us. Thus instead of the comically and tragically durable characteristics embedded deep in Molière's characters, character and its feelings are permeable and inconstant in many ways. Arlequin and Silvia, the main protagonists in *La Double inconstance*, do, nevertheless, appear to have acceded to the kind of constant and transparent relationship for which Rousseau yearns.

La Double inconstance (1723)

Silvia and Arlequin, the central characters of *La Double inconstance*, appear to enjoy a relationship built on an unquestionably mutual love. Simple and transparent, unswervingly trusting, they seem to withstand the pressures of opinion. This comedy begins as many end – with the prospects of a happy marriage. It is in fact not clear where the play will come from. Then, with as much melancholy as comedy, their love is dismantled and reconstructed in front of our eyes. As the title suggests, these lovers are ultimately wedded only by their common inconstancy.

In contrast to Figaro, Beaumarchais's great mover and shaker, Silvia and Arlequin attempt to resist any movement in the interests of preserving a happiness which is apparently beyond doubt. So when the prince, who wants the hand of Silvia, intercedes and tries to break up their relationship by means of different stratagems, they resist valiantly. Their ability to achieve constancy is, however, undermined not, as in the *Supplément au voyage de Bougainville*, by the assaults of a changing, pressuring world, but by an inherent instability dormant in the characters of Arlequin and Silvia. In both cases the intense autonomy of their feelings is checked and finally undermined by the opinions of others, which prey on the disturbing truth that self-love is the primary conduit for love.

Firstly, Silvia's vanity wins over her love when her self-worth is tested by the opinions of other women who, it is said, do not think much of Arlequin and laugh at her. Silvia's resistance to these opinions and her steadfast satisfaction with Arlequin, however, already betray a self-interested awareness of the regard of others. When she explains that she could not possibly give up Arlequin, she avers that, for one thing, her faithfulness to him makes her remarkable. After all, she says, 'cette fidélité n'est-elle pas mon charme?' (is not this fidelity my charm?). Her steadfast faithfulness to Arlequin actually glorifies her rather than him. Fidelity secures her the charm that would appear to be its opposite and she reveals a consciousness that her ability to be faithful increases all the more her opportunities to be unfaithful. This brushes a paradox that has teased us earlier. Already in act I, scene V, Arlequin has launched into rhapsodies which sing of Silvia's spectacularly admirable modesty. It does not take long for the opinions apparently shared by other women to convince Silvia that she can and must do better. And indeed, look! Silvia has fallen in love with the prince.

Arlequin loves Silvia with as impressive and intense a devotion. His love for her will not be budged by the promise of greater wealth and prestige which the prince offers him, but then, being a man, he begins to be won over when offered some particularly good food. But as avid as his stomach, Arlequin's self-love also effects the transfer of his affections from Silvia. The prince tries another tactic when the promise of wealth fails, and he invites a woman by the name of Flaminia to seduce Arlequin and thus deflect his attentions from Silvia. This effort is initially unsuccessful, but then Flaminia adroitly addresses Arlequin's self-love. She persuades Arlequin that he resembles a putative lost lover whom she laments, and it does not take long for Arlequin to reflect that: 'puisque vous aimiez tant ma copie, il faut bien croire que l'original mérite quelque chose' (since you liked my copy so much, one has every right to think that the original is worth something). Self-love flatters and affirms itself paradoxically through a derivative reliance on the opinions of others. Arlequin's self-love performs the trick of inverting the original and the copy, so that he appears to have preceded the copy and to have inspired the subsequent comparison and affection. Look! Arlequin has fallen in love with Flaminia.

Self-love is one of the chief ingredients of love. Our relationships with others are nourished by this force. Yet self-love is itself nurtured by the plural opinions of others. Our feelings are then left spinning in a circular motion. Having successfully induced Arlequin to forsake his love in order to reciprocate her sentiments, it is now not clear whether Flaminia truly feels or merely affects these sentiments. She herself appears to be confused: 'Je ne sais où je suis' (I don't know where I am) she confides, in a phrase that recalls the classic expression of disorientation in seventeenth-century tragic theatre: 'Où suis-je?' (where am I?). It is now not clear to us whether the self has been persuaded by love to become the persona this self was acting. The stage raises the question, as pertinently as travel literature does, when are we ever ourselves, when do we not perform for others? Where is an authentic self to be found? And it too suggests that language is not an innocent vehicle for our emotions but helps to delude us about them.

Arlequin decries the superficial mores of society and the worth-lessness of court life, and when Trivelin invokes fate in an attempt to convince him of the inevitability of his separation from Silvia, Arlequin dismisses this notion of predetermined hierarchies: 'Là-haut on n'écrit pas de telles impertinences' (up there no such impertinence is prescribed). Just as Arlequin refuses predestination he refuses to believe that physionomy can say anything about anyone.

However, Arlequin's consciousness of the fallacy of such arguments and the inadequacy of what they promise, does not persuade him to indulge in satire, let alone to lead a revolution. His indignation is directed not at overturning the upper orders but in justifying his lowly position. Silvia's pride, like that of Arlequin, is not composed in any part by envy or bothered by dynamism. As she declares 'Je demeure là, je ne vais ni ne viens' (I remain there, I neither go or come). The resistance to the superficial advantages enjoyed by the upper *échelons* of society does not permit a satirical view, but helps to account for their subsequent *volte-face* since, suspiciously, Arlequin takes a pride in his own humility, as Silvia is not unaware of the charms resident in her fidelity.

Many eighteenth-century writers couple a belief in the dynamism of man with a satire of the social privileges and religious predestination which thwart it. Here both the dynamism and the satire are muted in the interests of comedy induced by self-love and self-delusion. And in a later play, *Le Jeu de l'amour et du hasard*, this sense that the liberty of humans and the rights of our feelings are circumscribed by society is perhaps pronounced with further clarity.

Le Jeu de l'amour et du hasard (1730)

This play begins, as *La Double inconstance* does, with an apparent consensus which is not remotely disturbed by the traditional obstacles to love which interest playwrights, since Silvia has an obliging father and a nice husband, Dorante, lined up for her. However, Silvia is aware of the disparity between relationships in private and in public and wishes to be able to judge a private space unalloyed by the influences or demands of the public sphere. In her exposure of the duplicity of male behaviour flickers further satirical potential. In *La Double inconstance* an intense, unquestioned relationship between two lovers is carried into a social realm where it breaks up. In *Le Jeu de l'amour et du hasard*, conversely, the relationship between man and woman is known to be comfortable in social situations where the desire to interact harmoniously overwhelms any real tensions among the opinions of others, but Silvia is worried that, once transposed by marriage to the private, intimate space of the conjugal home, the affection displayed in society will not be sustained. Both comedies identify discrepancies between love in society and in privacy, but they illuminate them from different directions.

Silvia accordingly decides to speak to Dorante disguised as a servant in order to ascertain his real feelings. Dorante happens to have the same idea, while, in order to facilitate the ruse, their servants also disguise as their respective masters. Beneath the disguises their faces and their language betray their identities, and indeed these qualities are enhanced by being placed into a context which throws them into relief. They eventually recognise who they are. Social status is inscribed in body and in language, so that notwithstanding the title, any 'hasard' or chance is subordinate to the social truth that class will out.

Comedy moves inexorably towards the marriage that is its conclusion, but not before a transitional state of confusion. It is at the stage of coming to terms with one's desires and feelings that Marivaux's characters are arrested. Language does not belong to them but to their social environment. Hence their yearning for truths that are not susceptible to these influences but declare the truth plainly and simply. The prince observes in act III, scene 1 when commending Silvia's sincerity, 'ici, c'est le coeur tout pur qui parle' (here, it is the heart in all its purity that speaks). She achieves a sincerity and authenticity which are betrayed by the conventional discourses of most women. When she realises what is going on and that the charming servant before her is Dorante, Silvia achieves an immediate vision of the truth: 'Je vois clair dans mon coeur' (I see clearly into my heart). It is a moment of transparency and truth where the recesses of the heart and the mysteries of the inner self take precise visible form. Now restored to self-knowledge, Silvia becomes a sort of playwright herself and duly directs Dorante, manipulating him before finally revealing herself to him.

Desire and love are developed in part by our resistance to them, and it is the intercession of a third person (or a fourth and fifth) that concentrates knowledge of the self. Self-love and its life in society have been the object of diverse philosophical enquiries. With great subtlety Marivaux shows how self-love and love are produced and welded by the composite of conventions, interactions and opinions that we know as society. Marivaux' plays are not dominated by satire directed at the local characteristics of contemporary society, although later plays like *Les Fausses confidences* (1737) do chart the development of a certain mercantile culture. Unlike Molière's plays, the obstacles to the happiness of the younger characters are furnished by internal rather than external forces. Marivaux's characters are not mimetic. That is, their names and attributes are not supposed to be those of real people. They are above all what they say, a sum of linguistic traits. Marivaux's plays seem characterised by the paradox that their characters are modelled on the abstract types provided by the

Italian theatre, rather than being anchored in a specific social or biographical context, yet the love they share is never essential, but always indebted to a given social milieu. Nor do the archetypal characters of the *commedia dell'arte* which people Marivaux's theatre invite the satirical, topical readings that other eighteenth-century texts encourage. It should, nevertheless, be clear that these abstract types are constructed by their society and that many of the anxieties experienced by his characters and the subtleties with which they are brought to light situate them more closely to the overtly philosophical texts than might at first be supposed.

Marivaux's greatest foil is Pierre-Caron de Beaumarchais, the other incontestable genius of the eighteenth-century French theatre. In contrast to Marivaux, he pushes hard for reform and his plays, seen by some as a cause of the Revolution, have been read as documents that allude to and protest at specific events. But just as Marivaux's abstract characters discover the importance of social influences, so it is possible to move beyond the specificity of characters revealed by the x-rays of biographically minded critics to a more archetypal level where the human condition is at issue. It is in his comedy, *Le Mariage de Figaro*, that these different elements which enrich Beaumarchais's genius can best be appreciated.

3. Beaumarchais

Le Mariage de Figaro (1784)

If the world of Marivaux's comedies seems largely indifferent to the specificities of contemporary society and recent history, Beaumarchais's plays appear to revel in the exposure of the particular injustices which he sees there. It has proved possible to decode the characters in Beaumarchais's plays as figures in his own life or its wider historical context. And this is certainly what Louis XVI (who reigned from 1774 to 1792) supposed when he banned *Le Mariage de Figaro* from performance. Even if this comedy is set, at a safe distance, in Spain and the actors are to wear old-fashioned Spanish costumes, it was clear that it is levelled at the vices which prevail in contemporary France. Even the hero of the play, Figaro, whose name, like those of Marivaux's characters, seems to be a cipher which is not based on reality, was soon deciphered as Beaumarchais himself (whose real name was *fils* Caron or Caron the younger). Napoleon later called the play one of the causes of the Revolution. When the ban was lifted and this tantalisingly scandalous play was finally performed in 1784, the appetite of the public for the play had been whetted to such an extent that it became the most famous performance of the century. The audience was crowded so tightly that, apparently, at least one spectator was not only crushed to death, but left, wedged between others, for the duration of the play.

Whether or not we understand the particular context which gave birth to the play, *Le Mariage de Figaro* is still today highly interesting and great fun – provided, of course, that we do not die in the audience. This durable appeal is in part attributable to Beaumarchais's understanding of the eternal characteristics of human nature. Just as a specific message (about the fate of Lally-Tolendal) and a general truth (about mutable fortunes) both possibly inhabit David's painting of Belisarius, so Beaumarchais moves between the temporality of history and an eternal present in his plays. Beaumarchais directs his gaze not only at the injustices of the age but inwardly in a Rousseauesque fashion towards 'le coeur humain , qui a été, est et sera toujours le même' (the human heart which has been, is and will always be the same).

However, owing to the distracting possibilities of biography and the imminence of the Revolution we tend to forget this dimension to the play and look rather at its sources and its effects. Moreover, perhaps because the famous operas which are based on the Beaumarchais comedies, Mozart's *Le Nozze di Figaro* (1785) and Rossini's *Il Barbiere di Siviglia* (1817), invert the sequence in which they were written, we tend to forget that *Le Mariage de Figaro* lies at the centre of a trilogy. When considered alongside *Le Barbier de Séville* (1775) and *La Mère coupable* (1792), a different, perhaps more complex, vision of human nature is foregrounded. Although the plays span some twenty years and can be enjoyed in their own right, they were, Beaumarchais says, designed to be performed on successive nights, and it is profitable to see these plays as anticipations, corrections and developments of one

another. Like Marivaux, Beaumarchais deploys the same characters in different plays, but, unlike Marivaux, he exposes these
characters to the passage of time between one play and the next.
Beaumarchais is extremely skilful in sustaining a character over
different plays in a plausible, recognisable way, while still subjecting it to changes that are quite unforeseeable so, when this
character is seen in a new light, it is a light sparked in and connected by a previous play.

At the beginning of *Le Mariage de Figaro*, the young lovers,
Suzanne and Figaro, are cheerfully making plans for their wedding, but, it soon transpires that, although (or, in fact, because) he
is now married to Rosine, the Count has turned his attentions elsewhere. He therefore wishes to remove Figaro and lay claim to
Suzanne by invoking the *droit de seigneur*, an ancient right which
allows the lord of the manor to sleep with any woman from his
estate on the eve of her marriage. This is rather surprising, if we
recall *Le Barbier de Séville*, because in that play Figaro assisted the
Count in wresting Rosine from the hold of that walking anachronism, Bartholo, a Molièresque doctor let loose into a good
Enlightenment play, who had hoped to marry her. But now, disturbingly, the Count, Bartholo's adversary, takes over his dark
mantle, while, in a bizarre twist, the irredeemable Bartholo later
turns out to be Figaro's father.

Unlike the prince's efforts to get his girl in *La Double inconstance*
which seem destined to be rewarded and rewarding, the persistence of Bartholo and later the Count to do likewise is without
doubt the sinister expression of an absolutist force. Rosine, who
married the dashing Count after the happy ending to *Le Barbier de
Séville*, now laments the failure of their relationship. When some
eighteenth-century works became operas, their intricacies were traduced in saccharine, if delightful versions (the *Manon Lescaut* of of
Jules Massenet (1884) and Giacomo Puccini (1893) or Francesco
Cilea's *Adriana Lecouvreur* (1902) come to mind), but it was the
good fortune of *Le Mariage de Figaro* to find a librettist and a composer, Lorenzo Da Ponte and Mozart, who were sympathetic to the
nuances of Beaumarchais's writing and the tragedy which skirts his
comedy. Rosina's wistful evocation of lost happiness in the aria
'Dove sono i bei momenti?' (where have all the good times gone?)

tells us with beautiful poignancy that if comedies end in marriage, tragedies seem to begin with it.

Happily, thanks to a fortuitous, often curious succession of events, the marriage of Figaro to Suzanne can at length take place. In *Le Barbier de Séville*, the wit and ingenuity of Figaro won the day. But if, here too, the intelligence of Figaro and Suzanne engineer a victory over folly and injustice that looks inevitable, the obstacles which they must overcome are more intractable. Whereas the twists and turns of the previous play were unpredictable but fore-seeable (at least by Figaro), events are now simply bizarre. Not only are they unpredictable, but, having occurred, they remain inexplicable. Even to Figaro. He is now upstaged by the young figure, Chérubin, neither child nor man, Rosine's mischievous page. The escalation in the complexity of the plays and the increasing uncertainty of the characters can be measured by looking at two Figaro speeches from the first two plays of the trilogy. When, in the first act of *Le Barbier de Séville*, the Count asks Figaro what he has been up to, he gets more than he bargained for:

Voyant à Madrid que la république des lettres était celle des loups, toujours armés les uns contre les autres, et que, livrés au mépris où ce risible acharnement les conduit, tous les insectes, les moustiques, les cousins, les critiques, les maringouins, les envieux, les feuillistes, les libraires, les censeurs, et tout ce qui s'attache à la peau des malheureux gens de lettres, achevait de déchiqueter et sucer le peu de substance qui leur restait; fatigué d'écrire, ennuyé de moi, dégoûté des autres, abîmé de dettes et léger d'argent; à la fin, convaincu que l'utile revenu du rasoir est préférable aux vains honneurs de la plume, j'ai quitté Madrid, et, mon bagage en sautoir, parcourant philosophiquement les deux Castilles, la Manche, l'Estramadure, la Sierra-Morena, l'Andalousie; accueilli dans une ville, emprisonné dans l'autre, et partout supérieur aux événements;

(Having formed the impression that the literary world in Madrid was largely inhabited by wolves, hunting each other in packs, and as you would expect, given all the ridiculous ripping and tearing that goes on, all the swarms of miserable insects, mosquitoes, midges, critics, horseflies, mean-minded little hacks, journalists, publishers,

censors and all the other bloodsuckers that attach themselves to
writers, God help them, had done lacerating them and sucked them
dry of any last drop of red blood they might have ever possessed;
sick of writing, boring even myself, disgusted by everyone else, up to
the eyes in debt and not a sniff of money; in the end, coming to the
conclusion that a steady income from pulling a razor is preferable
to the unpaid distinction of pushing a pen, I left Madrid, slung my
bag over my shoulder and tramped very happily through every
province in the country; Castile, La Mancha, Extremadura, Sierra
Morena, ending up in Andalusia; in one place they greeted me with
open arms, the next they locked me up: wherever I went I rose
above it;)

Figaro's metaphors portray a world where authors are subject to
a swarm of figures that interfere between them and their readers.
The metaphor, initially reasonably familiar, seems to acquire a self-
generating force of its own, as it outgrows its purpose and becomes
grotesquely graphic. Suddenly, in the midst of this swarm of
insects, critics are mentioned. Their presence seems to literalise
the other metaphors, because we will have thought they were referring metaphorically to critics. Critics might seem out of place
among this swarm of insects, but they have been summoned by the
rhyming 'moustiques'. Like a flea, the rhyme hops across different
categories and authorises the jump from one meaning to another.
It is characteristic of Figaro's verve in which he changes the
meaning of words and their relations and references. This is one
of the ways he succeeds in being subversive. Just as Figaro keeps
changing jobs and moving places, so linguistically he is dynamic in
liberating words from their usual meanings and turning fixed
truths on their head.

Figaro's travels recollected in *Le Barbier de Séville* resemble a
quixotic picaresque journey, but the fatigue and disenchantment
to which he is subject sound a serious note within the comedy. The
hero's enemies are not the traditionally ridiculous enemies of the
Enlightenment, but injustices which divide authors from one
another and doubts which cut Figaro from himself. However,
beneath all this turmoil the phrase 'supérieur aux événements'
rings out. After all Figaro retains an Enlightenment understanding

of one's environment, and, better still, a capacity to master it.

This speech provides an interesting foil to the more sombre and introspective soliloquy in act V, scene 3 of *Le Mariage de Figaro*. Whereas this speech is a protracted answer to an enquiry, here Figaro gloomily gives voice to an inner anguish. Deluded that Suzanne has a tryst with the Count, he launches into an extremely long and embittered speech, first lamenting the frailty of woman and then bemoaning the injustices of life:

(*Il retombe assis*) O bizarre suite d'événements! Comment cela m'est-il arrivé? Pourquoi ces choses et non pas d'autres? Qui les a fixées sur ma tête? Forcé de parcourir la route où je suis entré sans le savoir, comme j'en sortirai sans le vouloir, je l'ai jonchée d'autant de fleurs que ma gaieté me l'a permis; encore je dis ma gaieté, sans savoir si elle est à moi plus que le reste, ni même quel est ce *moi* dont je m'occupe: un assemblage informe de parties inconnues; puis un chétif être imbécile; un petit animal folâtre; un jeune homme ardent au plaisir, ayant tous les goûts pour jouir, faisant tous les métiers pour vivre; maître ici, valet là, selon qu'il plaît à la fortune!

((*He sits down again*) What an amazing sequence of events! How did all that happen to me? Why those things and not others? Who was it said it must be me? Forced to travel a road I came upon without knowing it, that I shall leave without wanting to, I've scattered as many rosebuds as my natural optimism has permitted. There again, I say my natural optimism without knowing if it's mine any more than the rest is...nor even what this *me* is that I'm so concerned about: a little shapeless bundle of undiscovered mysteries, then a poor little imbecile of a creature, a little playful animal, a young man who'll do anything for pleasure, with every appetite to enjoy, doing any work to live: a master here, a servant there, as blind chance decides!)

Even if it is occasioned by an illusory feeling, Figaro's soliloquy is informed by a genuine angst about the self and the tribulations to which it is subject. This autobiography is much less particularised than that provided in his speech in *Le Barbier de Séville*. It asks more agonised questions about human existence. He is no longer worried about being penniless and sucked of his blood but worries about a more fundamental dispossession. What belongs properly to the self, this purely material 'assemblage informe de parties inconnues', and what are its powers in the world? His travels are no longer down the winding roads of Spain but the road of life itself on which, prefiguring Sade's vocabulary in *La Philosophie dans le boudoir*, he has strewn flowers. Far from being 'partout supérieur aux événements', he can only conclude that he is at fortune's mercy. Indeed, the awareness of this passivity causes him to sit down and to check his dynamism. He is unable to act. In this soliloquy pronounced 'dans l'obscurité' (in the dark) his independence has turned into solitude. He has evolved from existing as the generic valet figure known cheerfully as 'le Barbier' to being his own man, Figaro. If his name is entirely his own, he also feels entirely alone.

This is the second long and highly deliberative soliloquy of the play. In act III Marceline launches into a tirade about the treatment of women. Its sheer length means that it is frequently omitted from stage performance. The coherence of the action and the illusion of comedy is punctured not only by these long soliloquies, but disturbed by a seemingly uncontrollable mass of comic scenes. *Le Mariage de Figaro* is no doubt one of the most interesting plays of the eighteenth century, in part because it is of all of them the most anarchic. Beaumarchais manipulates all imaginable stock devices, people hiding in cupboards, going up and down ladders, discovering their parents, with consummate skill. But these are all embroidered with a poignant, semi-tragic vision. This exhibition of self-conscious artifice transmits the sense that life is bearable only if we laugh at it, which is a sad notion. Indeed Figaro admits in *Le Barbier de Séville* that 'je me presse de rire de tout, de peur d'être obligé d'en pleurer' (I'm very quick to laugh at anything for fear that it might make me cry).

Through all these vicissitudes, wit and intelligence, nevertheless, remain militant and emerge triumphant over injustice. Just as the chance of *Le Jeu de l'amour et du hasard* is subordinate to an inevitable match, so here the madness of 'la folle journée' is finally defeated by good sense. In some cases, Marivaux's protagonists try to slow down change which will only dizzy and unsettle them.

Beaumarchais's heroes cannot wait for it. As Suzanne declares, 'l'esprit seul peut tout changer' (only intelligence can change everything). However, this assurance is qualified by Figaro's grateful, bemused remark towards the end of the play that 'le hasard a mieux fait que nous' (chance has done better than us). The play is then not only a monument to Enlightenment optimism but a record of human fallibility. Although the satirical pungency with which the barber cuts down his enemies is still visible in *Le Mariage de Figaro*, it is accompanied by a disturbing feeling that the happiness which was acquired with such art in *Le Barbier de Séville* is yet harder to retain. The misdemeanours of the past that the barber sought to rectify still linger. And an uncertain future, rendered all the more uncertain by our knowledge that even the happy ending of the *Le Barbier de Séville* turned out to be provisional, lodges in this happy ending. 'Tout finit-it par chanson' (everything finish-shes in a song) sings Brid'oison at the very end. But it is a truth not only sung but stuttered.

L'Autre Tartuffe, ou la mère coupable (1792)

This uncertain future finds expression in the final play of the trilogy, *L'Autre Tartuffe, ou la mère coupable*, which, first performed during the Revolution in 1792, has never attracted the attention it deserves. The scene opens shrouded in inauspiciously dark colours. An autumnal mood reigns. The Countess is, mysteriously, in mourning as she is every year on this day, the feast of Saint Leo (November 10th). It duly becomes clear that she is mourning Chérubin, with whom she had an affair and by whom she has had a child. In order to expiate this crime, he joined the army and died, gratefully, in service. The drama which ensues traces the way this secret becomes known to the Count and the way their illegitimate children, Léon and Florestine, can then marry without fear of incest. Attempting to thwart this sucessful outcome is an odious schemer by the name of Bégearss, who insinuates himself into the household and therefore earns the additional name of the 'new Tartuffe', after the hypocritical villain of Molière's play, *Le Tartuffe* (1664).

Beaumarchais salutes the changes which have occurred in the

Revolution with an abundance of references to divorce, changes in titles and a bust of George Washington, among others. The play is not a comedy but a drama which responds to an edict in Diderot's dialogue, the *Entretien sur le fils naturel* (1757), that playwrights should remove servants from the stage and concentrate rather on children and families. Figaro's role is further marginalised as Rosine and the Count learn to confide in their children. The comedy of the child finding his parents is supplanted by the poignancy of the parents learning who their children are, and who they themselves are.

The most striking change of all is the transfer of the scene from Spain to France. We soon learn that the Count's property in Spain, 'Aguas frescas' or Clear Waters, has been sold and converted into shares in the New World. This revelation is one of those telling moments when the wig is removed, signalling the change to an age where fixed hierarchies no longer rest in place but are converted into a new and liquid economy. Again, the Enlightenment might be seen to have triumphed. But you have been warned that beneath the wig lies a sight which is not always agreeable. Even in its anxiety to conform to the new rhythms of the age, the play cannot hide some wistful retrospection. The Count's estate and regime in *Le Mariage de Figaro* were without doubt unreasonable. But, redolent rather of the utopian 'Clarens' in Rousseau's *Julie* than of château Thunder-ten-Tronck from which Voltaire's Candide departs, 'Aguas frescas' sounds natural, vital and agreeable. This 'château en Espagne' (castle in Spain), the French term for a castle in the air, was, by comparison, a fantasy, an idyll. Although corruption prevailed there, the characters knew what to expect and how to live with it, but the clear waters of 'Aguas frescas' have now been muddied by the frustrations of uncertainty. As Olympe de Gouges remarks, vice seemed to suggest its own remedy, and the new world cleansed of the injustices of the ancien Régime is without the clarity and much of the interest of the imperfect society it has replaced.

Without doubt the nostalgia and melancholy which linger over the play are fuelled by the death of Chérubin. Since there has been a gradual accretion of characters throughout the trilogy, the absence of Chérubin from its final part is all the more disturbing.

He is the only character who escapes the process of ageing. Neither child nor man, both man and woman (indeed he is played by a woman), both innocently cherubic and potentially *libertin*, Chérubin in *Le Mariage de Figaro* is the figure onto whom all the other characters project their own memories and regrets. Never committed to a fixed position, Chérubin represents the impossible coalescence of opposites, youth and age, music and morality, women and men, that Beaumarchais would wish to reconcile in his theatre. But only in their absence can these opposites be fulfilled and retained. Chérubin embodies a truth which is salutary as it is tragic: our potential is always greater than our achievements. Chérubin's death is also that of an age in which innocence and evil were somehow reconcilable. He is left behind by the Revolution, preserving the savour of an age that is both objectionable and desirable.

If the trilogy opens with the Count looking impatiently at his watch and trying to get time to move on, here there is an attempt to slow it down. The trilogy is a sustained reflection on time. The victory at the end of *Le Barbier de Séville* was trumpeted as the inevitable triumph of youth over age, rather than celebrating more portentously the defeat by right of wrong. In its final words, Figaro declares: 'quand la jeunesse et l'amour sont d'accord pour tromper un vieillard, tout ce qu'il fait pour l'empêcher peut bien s'appeler à bon droit *la Précaution inutile*' (when youth and love agree to deceive an old man, all he does can with great reason be called *the Useless Precaution*). Youth vanquishes age, as Enlightenment overcomes the ancien regime. But having overcome age, youth had to become it. This process reveals the development of internal obstacles and a loss of the confidence and brightness that were previously evident. Finally, however, the struggle between generations is reconciled within the character of Figaro: 'O ma vieillesse! pardonne à ma jeunesse, elle s'honorera de toi' (I hope as an old man I can forgive myself for what I did when I was younger). This reconciliation of young and old selves within Figaro bridges the agonising gaps between generations that the Revolution had stretched even further.

La Mère coupable ends happily. Thanks to a final flash of his old ingenuity, Figaro can save the day, since there is no interceding king nor any need for one to defeat the new Tartuffe (as there had been in Molière's play). The new Tartuffe fails to take the money, so the play ends as a triumph of solvency if not love. In the final moments of this last scene the grateful Count offers Figaro a financial reward which he turns down. This rejection signals either Figaro's acquisition of autonomy and self-confidence or perhaps his willingness to stick to a more traditional model of loyalty which precedes the reign of money. It is a rejoinder at any rate to Molière. If the ghost of Tartuffe hangs over the play, that of Don Juan incarnated by the figure of the Count is also expelled. As Molière's Don Juan is transported to Hell at the end of the play, Sganarelle, his servant, cries out in despair that everything has been rightfully restored to order except his wages. Figaro ensures emphatically that even self-interest is tractable in front of loyalty and that we have at last acceded to a world no longer defined by passion and caprice but duty and virtue. This drama too can now end in marriage, but the *dénouement* of the play also projects, like David's painting, a union of different generations, as it closes, through the timeless virtues of honesty and compassion, the gap between the ancien regime past and the post-Revolutionary present.

*

Each of Beaumarchais's plays seeks to register the particular characteristics of the age in and about which it is written and it attempts to find the form, be it comedy or tragedy, that corresponds. But the trilogy teaches us also that, for all the radical differences between generations present and past, the universal and eternal insufficiencies of man remain in common to them. Beaumarchais's plays suggest that the difficulties their characters experience are in part local and removable by the conviction of reason, but the recurrence of Molière's Tartuffe character in the figure of Bégearss suggests that, even in a new age, imperfections remain embedded in human existence. From *Le Barbier de Séville* to *La Mère coupable* we are transported, with considerable stuttering on the way, between radically different models of theatre and visions of society, from the excitement of courtship to the traumas of infidelity. Cuckoldry, the subject cherished by many comedies of the ancien regime, has made way for the more introspective enquiries into adultery that would be a mainstay of the nineteenth-century novel.

La Mère coupable takes us again into the heart of the Revolution. Just as Olympe de Gouges sees the Revolution as promising new opportunities but delivering painful disappointment, so Beaumarchais (elected as a leader but then exiled from France under the Revolution) views it as responsible both for new terrors and new beginnings. Literature of the Revolutionary period tends to move in one of two opposing directions; either it congratulates itself on its relation to history or it removes itself in the interests of a new and intense introspection from the arena. These years of unprecedented turmoil and violence both encourage and threaten different literary endeavours.

Selected Reading

Geoffrey Bremner, 'An interpretation of Diderot's *Paradoxe sur le comédien*', *British Journal of Eighteenth-Century Studies*, 4 (1981), 28-43. Stimulating analysis of the dialogue and its implications.

D.J. Culpin, *Marivaux and Reason: A Study in Early Enlightenment Thought* (New York: Peter Lang, 1993). A work which restores the importance of Marivaux as a thinker by looking at both plays and novels by Marivaux.

William D. Howarth, *Beaumarchais and the Theatre* (London: Routledge, 1995). An exhaustive study of Beaumarchais's plays and theories which sidesteps a lot of the biographical readings of the plays in an effort to see how they work on the stage.

John Hope Mason, 'The *Lettre à d'Alembert* and its place in Rousseau's Thought', in *Rousseau and the Eighteenth Century*, ed. by Marian Hobson et al (Oxford: Oxford University Press, 1992), pp. 251-69. A study of the *Lettre à d'Alembert* in relation to his political and philsophical ideas.

John McManners, *Abbés and Actresses: The Church and the Theatrical Profession in Eighteenth-Century France* (Oxford: Oxford University Press, 1986). A study of antitheatrical prejudice in the eighteenth century.

David Marshall, *The Surprising Effects of Sympathy: Marivaux, Diderot, Rousseau and Mary Shelley* (London; Chicago: University of Chicago

Press, 1988). A wide-ranging but incisive study of problems concerning theatricality which contains chapters on the *Lettre à d'Alembert* and the *Paradoxe sur le comédien.*

Jeffrey S. Ravel, *The Contested Parterre: Public Theater and French Political Culture, 1680-1791* (Cornell: Cornell University Press, 1999). A work which looks at the composition of theatre audiences and the political influence exerted by the stage in the period.

Paul Robinson, *Opera and Ideas* (Stanford: Stanford University Press, 1985). An interesting study of the adaptations of Beaumarchais's plays by Mozart and Rossini which is more responsive to their qualities than those of the plays.

IX

Writing in the Revolution

On July 14th 1789, the Bastille was stormed and the French Revolution was under way. It would rage for ten years, threatening and usually destroying all possible conceptions and assumptions on a scale never seen before. It simply was *the* Revolution. In 1792 a first French Republic was declared and the calendar revised so that it became Year I. Its twelve months, all of thirty days, bore new names suggested by the seasons. Never mind the millennium, the Revolution now provided an opportunity to start afresh, to locate and adhere to purely natural and rational bases. The writers and thinkers of the Enlightenment had, in their different ways, yearned for a new start, whether that afforded by the 'New World' or that enviably contrived by the seventeenth-century genius. In the *Prelude* (begun in 1798-99) Wordsworth recounted the exultation with which he welcomed the Revolution in these rapturous lines: 'Bliss was it that dawn to be alive/But to be young was very Heaven'. Olympe de Gouges, likewise, views the Revolution as a dawn which, frustratingly, woman has overslept, when sounding her call, 'Femme, réveille-toi' (woman, wake up). But to be old during the Revolution was Hell for some people. Wordsworth's dawn is a twilight for Beaumarchais and most of the characters in *La Mère coupable* which, although first performed in Year I, is dominated by the rhythms of the Christian calendar and haunted by thoughts of the past. For the poet André Chénier, who wrote his *Iambe* beginning 'Comme un dernier rayon, comme un dernier zéphyre/Animent la fin d'un beau jour' (as a last ray of sunlight, a last breeze animates the end of a beautiful day) as he awaited his execution, it is also definitely evening.

André Chénier, Iambes, XI: *'Comme un dernier rayon...' (1794)*

André Chénier was born in 1762 in Constantinople, where his father was the French consul. His mother claimed to be of Greek descent. A love of antiquity pervades Chénier's poetry. In his *Bucoliques* (1785-87), he sets about reviving the pastoral genres which had been discredited since the assaults of Voltaire and others. Chénier heralds a rebirth of poetry with his belief in the regenerative, creative force of the poet. Anticipating Romantic conceptions of the artist, he declares in his *Elégies,* 'L'art ne fait que des vers, le coeur seul est poète' (art only writes verse, the heart alone is the poet). In contrast to the ideas recommended by Premier in Diderot's *Le Paradoxe sur le comédien,* the heart is the supreme agent. Chénier represents a final eighteenth-century effort to articulate immediate truths from the soul that is the seat of intuition and inspiration, as philosophers, deists and writers have before him in the century.

Written on a tiny scrap of paper as he languished in the prison of Saint-Lazare prior to his execution on 7 Thermidor, Year II (25th July, 1794), Chénier's final poem is not only a 'cri de coeur', the anguished final words of a condemned man, but a remarkable statement about injustice and the writer's stand against it. This amalgam of lyricism and invective (satirical abuse) typifies the different directions that writing takes during and after the Revolution, as writers feel at once empowered by an event which is influenced by eloquence, and overtaken by the violence which this event unleashes.

> Comme un dernier rayon, comme un dernier zéphyre
> Animent la fin d'un beau jour,
> Au pied de l'échafaud j'essaye encore ma lyre.
> Peut-être est-ce bientôt mon tour.
> Peut-être avant que l'heure en cercle promenée
> Ait posé sur l'émail brillant,
> Dans les soixante pas où sa route est bornée,
> Son pied sonore et vigilant,
> Le sommeil du tombeau pressera ma paupière.

Avant que de ses deux moitiés
Ce vers que je commence ait atteint la dernière,
Peut-être en ces murs effrayés
Le messager de mort, noir recruteur des ombres,
Escorté d'infâmes soldats,
branlant de mon nom ces longs corridors sombres,
Où seul dans la foule à grands pas
J'erre, aiguisant ces dards persécuteurs du crime,
Du juste trop faibles soutiens,
Sur mes lèvres soudain va suspendre la rime;
Et chargeant mes bras de liens,
Me traîner amassant en foule à mon passage
Mes tristes compagnons reclus,
Qui me connaissaient tous avant l'affreux message,
Mais qui ne me connaissent plus.
Eh bien! j'ai trop vécu. Quelle franchise auguste,
De mâle constance et d'honneur
Quels exemples sacrés, doux à l'âme du juste,
Pour lui quelle ombre de bonheur,
Quelle Thémis terrible aux têtes criminelles,
Quels pleurs d'une noble pitié,
Des antiques bienfaits quels souvenirs fidèles,
Quels beaux échanges d'amitié,
Font digne de regrets l'habitacle des hommes?
La peur fugitive est leur Dieu;
La bassesse; la feinte. Ah! Lâches que nous sommes
Tous, oui, tous. Adieu, terre, adieu.
Vienne, vienne la mort! – Que la mort me délivre!
Ainsi donc mon coeur abattu
Cède aux poids de ses maux? Non, non. Puissé-je vivre!
Ma vie importe à la vertu.
Car l'honnête homme enfin, victime de l'outrage,
Dans les cachots, près du cercueil,
Relève plus altiers son front et son langage,
Brillants d'un généreux orgueil.
S'il est écrit aux cieux que jamais une épée
N'étincellera dans mes mains,
Dans l'encre et l'amertume une autre arme trempée

Peut encore servir les humains.
[...]
O ma plume! Fiel, bile, horreur, Dieux de ma vie!
Par vous seuls je respire encore:
Comme la poix brûlante agitée en ses veines
Ressuscite un flambeau mourant,
Je souffre; mais je vis. Par vous loin de mes peines,
D'espérance un vaste torrent
Me transporte. Sans vous, comme un poison livide,
L'invisible dent du chagrin,
Mes amis opprimés, du menteur homicide
Le succès, le sceptre d'airain;
Des bons proscrits par lui la mort ou la ruine,
L'opprobre de subir sa loi,
Tout eût tari ma vie; ou contre ma poitrine
Dirigé mon poignard. Mais quoi!
Nul ne resterait donc pour attendrir l'histoire
Sur tant de justes massacrés?
Pour consoler leurs fils, leurs veuves, leur mémoire,
Pour que des brigands abhorrés
Frémissent aux portraits noirs de leur ressemblance,
Pour descendre jusqu'aux enfers
Nouer le triple fouet, le fouet de la vengeance,
Déjà levé sur ces pervers?
Pour cracher sur leurs noms, pour chanter leur supplice?
Allons, étouffe tes clameurs;
Souffre, ô coeur gros de haine, affamé de justice.
Toi, Vertu, pleure si je meurs.

(Like a last ray of sunlight, like a last breeze which animate the end of a beautiful day, at the foot of the scaffold I shall yet try my lyre. Perhaps it will soon be my turn. Perhaps before the hour, having completed its round of sixty steps, has placed its sonorous and vigilant foot upon the shining enamel, the sleep of the tomb will shut my eyelids. Before I complete the second half of this line which I start, perhaps within these frightened walls the harbinger of death, the dark recruiter of the shadows, escorted by evil soldiers, making the long dark corridors resonate with my name, there where alone in the crowd I wander with great strides and sharpen my arrows which persecute crime, the too feeble support of good people, the rhyme will suddenly be interrupted on my lips; and fettering my arms with chains, they drag me through a crowd of my sad reclusive companions, who all knew me before the dreadful message but who know me no longer. Well then! I have lived too long. What noble frankness, what sacred examples of virile constancy and honour, tender to the heart of the just person, for him what a shadow of happiness, what a terrible Themis with criminal heads, what tears of a noble pity, what faithful memories of ancient benefits, what sublime exchanges of friendship make the habitations of men worth regretting? Transient fear is their God; baseness; deception. Oh! How cowardly we are, all of us, yes, all of us. Farewell, earth, farewell. Come to me, come to me, death! May death release me! So is my dejected heart thus giving way to the weight of the evils it bears? No, no. That I might live! My life is vital to virtue. For, after all, the good man, victim of injustice, in the dungeons, at death's door, lifts up his brow and his words with greater nobility. They gleam with generous pride. If it is written up above that a sword shall never gleam in my hands, then another arm drenched in ink and acrimony can yet be of service to the human race [...] O my pen! Gall, bile, horror, Gods of my life! Through you alone I still breathe: Like burning pitch moving through my veins a dying flame is resurrecting; I suffer, but I live. Through you a vast torrent of hope transports me far from my pains. Without you, like a livid poison, the invisible fang of chagrin, my oppressed friends, the triumph of the lying murderers, the sceptre of bronze; the good people condemned by it to death or ruin or to the insult of having to follow its law, all this would have sapped me of life or would have persuaded me to stab myself. But what! No-one would remain then to soften the story of so many just people who have been massacred? No-one to console their sons, their widows, their legacy, so that the execrable bandits learn to shudder at the black portraits of them? No-one to descend into hell to tie up the triple scourge, the scourge of vengeance, already raised against these degenerates? No-one to spit upon their names, to sing of their suffering? Let's away, quieten these shouts; suffer, O heart swelled by hatred, hungry for justice. And You, virtue, cry if I die.)

Chénier's evocation of the setting sun as a beautiful day nears its end provides a conciliatory start to the poem. The poet savours the final moments of light; his two similes in the opening alexandrine (line of 12 syllables) seem tranquil, even leisurely. Although the allusion to the scaffold is alarming, death (poetically translated as night here) is not made to sound grievous. The tentative 'j'essaye encore ma lyre', followed by the repeated 'peut-êtres' of the next lines, suggest acquiescence rather than anger, as he concentrates his poetic powers in order to produce what might be a final, lyrical rhapsody. The poet envisages death's arrival in a tender image: 'Le sommeil du tombeau pressera ma paupière'. The subjects responsible for his fate are the inevitable companions of man, 'l'heure' and 'le sommeil'. The poem is, however, gradually invaded by more sinister and particular harbingers of death as lyricism loses itself in the 'longs corridors sombres' of line fifteen. The poem becomes increasingly bilious as apparent exclamations ('Quels exemples sacrés...') turn out to be questions. It is, nevertheless, not too surprising a little later that he seems to accept his fate gracefully, even willingly: 'Adieu, terre, adieu. Vienne, vienne la mort! Que la mort me délivre!'

However, there then follows a violent recoil from this acceptance and invitation of death, and the poet, as though suddenly remarking that he does not need to die and that this is all dreadfully unfair, now launches into what seems a different poem: 'non, non, puissé-je vivre! Ma vie importe à la vertu'. But if we reread the previous lines it possibly becomes clear that they do foresee what follows. The very terms with which his departure was announced suggest reluctance. The repetition of 'adieu' emphasises a lingering wish to stay rather than the finality of a departure, while the urgency of the repeated 'Vienne, vienne la mort' likewise seems to stall the appearance of death even as it asks for it. Indeed, from its prominent position in the line, the 'vie' embedded in the subjunctive of 'venir' predominates over the 'mort' which twice cannot answer it convincingly.

These repetitions have the function of slowing down the time which comes to claim him with horrible haste. Where we saw leisurely, poetic imagery, we can now see a desire to forestall the terror and the blankness of death by writing. The lines which speculate about the passage of time and the imminence of his death are extremely long and complex, as though their author were terrified of what lies beyond the full stop. As long as he can write, he feels as safe as Scheherazade.

The remaining lines suggest that the pen can save the lives of others too. The poet no longer merely tries or hopes. Offering itself instead of the sword, the pen can, indeed will, protect and injure with great might: 'O ma plume! Fiel, bile, horreur, Dieux de ma vie!/ Par vous seuls je respire encore'. The juxtaposition of these incongruous terms pays tribute to the terrible power the pen can wield. The pen is not only a God that moves ('attendrir') and consoles ('consoler') but a God that travels to Hell ('jusqu'aux enfers') to take pleasure in the suffering of malefactors. The lyricism at the beginning of the poem has been eclipsed by a vision of the poet's vocation which engages him, urgently and violently, as spokesman against the particular injustices of the present. The heart which makes the poet ('le coeur seul est poète' is Chénier's credo) is not degraded but ennobled and swelled by such violent hatred: 'ô coeur gros de haine' he sings in the penultimate verse. So, amid the bilious satire directed at the horrors of contemporary life about him, an inner poetic purity remains intact. It returns, beautifully and momentarily, at the end:

Toi, Vertu, pleure si je meurs.

The 'si' or 'if', on which he pins the hope that he might survive, is finally deluged in the beautiful internal rhymes of 'pleure' and 'meurs'. After the long, often tortuous preceding phrases, this verse falls with the finality of the blade, and the simple brevity of the line seems to say that death is not a possibility, but now a reality.

*

If Voltaire's *Le Mondain* was written in the pallid dawn of an age emerging from the previous century, the sun now seems to have set over the Enlightenment. One poem rejoices in heaven on earth. The other curses hell on it. Chénier does not mince his words when considering the savagery and chaos of the age which has condemned him. But, just as Voltaire's poem takes an almost insolent pride in its form and style, so, even as he dies, the writer remains defiant here. The poem's celebration of the power of the writer is inspiring and terrifying. Its sudden shift from gently lyrical, timeless images to rousing and disturbing scenes forces us to read the poem differently. Like the painting of Belisarius, it reminds us of the squalor and injustice in life, but it evokes, at the same time, the beauty and dignity of the human condition.

It might be thought inevitable that, during the Revolution, action would overcome the writing which was perceived in some quarters to have been its stimulus. Literature written during the Revolution seems to suffer and pale alongside the compelling events of its history. But, as Chénier's poem shows, the confidence of the writer remained intact even in this period. With his cry of 'J'écris pour agir' (I write in order to act), Voltaire had set the standard for the 'écrivain engagé' (engaged writer), committed to political reform and action through his writing. The Revolution instituted, for the first time in France, freedom of the press. Many journals sprang up and attracted a plethora of new writers ardently committed to particular causes. Equally, the growth of assemblies and clubs promoted eloquence among speakers such as the comte de Mirabeau (1749-91) and Pierre-Victurnien Vergniaud (1753-93), who were adept at wooing large gatherings. Charles Rouget de Lisle (1760-1820), who had written numerous forgotten plays and poems, finally found his voice when, in 1792, he wrote the rousing words, 'Allons enfants de la patrie/ Le jour de gloire est arrivé' (Let us march, children of the nation/ The day of glory has arrived), and *La Marseillaise* was born.

However, the post-revolutionary period developed, perhaps as a reaction against these trends, a taste for more personal forms of writing which can be called autotelic because there is no aim or end other than that of writing. Rousseau was championed and sanctified by the Revolution because of his political theories, but, increasingly, it is the posthumously published personal works which resonate. It is therefore a dual legacy of Revolution and reverie that the eighteenth leaves to the nineteenth century. With his motto, 'sapere aude' (dare to know), Immanuel Kant captures the spirit of the Enlightenment, as it liberated itself from outmoded ways of thought. But, as it has been said, the Kantian injunction 'Dare to think for oneself' soon turned to 'Dare to write for oneself'.

Selected Reading

Keith Michael Baker, *Inventing the French Revolution* (Cambridge: Cambridge University Press, 1990). A series of challenging essays which includes sections on the 'language of politics' and the 'Revolutionary lexicon'.

Roger Chartier, *The Cultural Origins of the French Revolution* (Durham NC: Duke University Press, 1991). An examination of the changes in literary culture which precede the Revolution.

Malcolm Cook, 'Politics in the Fiction of the French Revolution, 1789-1794', *Studies on Voltaire and the Eighteenth Century*, 201 (1982), 235-340.

Graham Rodmell, *French Drama of the Revolutionary Years* (London: Routledge, 1990). An interesting book, notwithstanding its conclusion that there are no first-rate plays in this period.

Francis Scarfe, *André Chénier. His Life and Work 1762-1794* (Oxford: Oxford University Press, 1965. The authoritative study of Chénier's poems in their biographical context.

X

Conclusions

'Dis la chose comme elle est' (say it as it is), implores the implied reader of *Jacques le fataliste*. Certain eighteenth-century writers and their readers set off in search of Enlightenment with the confidence that truths are available and that they can be useful, provided enough concerted and careful effort is invested. Voltaire's 'Ingénu', for instance, enjoys the privilege of being someone who 'voyait les choses comme elles sont' (saw things as they are). However, the reader's demand for truths, our request for enlightenment, is more often exposed as futile and presumptuous.

Different visions of Enlightenment have offered themselves across a wide range of intellectual pursuits: Rousseau's panoramic view of the achievements of the human mind celebrated at the opening of his first discourse; The Premier's validation of reason in Diderot's *Paradoxe sur le comédien* ('C'est sa tête qui fait tout'); Suzanne's recommendation of the transforming power of intelligence ('l'esprit seul peut tout changer') in Beaumarchais's *Le Mariage de Figaro*. However, they seem to function ironically and are opposed, if not defeated, by their context. The light that eighteenth-century writers try to shed on their world is of many different shades: the prisms of Newtonian light, the strange aura of those like Belisarius who are denied light, the glare of Enlightenment irony, the crepuscular colours of Chénier's evening, the glint in the blade of the guillotine. When Virginie, in Bernardin de Saint-Pierre's story, dies, she is transfigured into pure light. It is perhaps characteristic of the eighteenth century that such an image of transcendence, or an appeal to truths beyond a changing, confusing world, should nonetheless remain loyal to the more scientific spirit of the Enlightenment, for it is to a particle of light, rather than a more mysterious nimbus, that she is compared.

In a passage towards the end of the text, the 'vieillard' assures her mournful lover Paul that Virginie is now happy:

> Virginie maintenant est heureuse. Ah! Si du séjour des anges elle pouvait se communiquer à vous, elle vous dirait, comme dans ses adieux: 'O Paul! La vie n'est qu'une épreuve. J'ai été trouvée fidèle aux lois de la nature, de l'amour et de la vertu [...] Le ciel a trouvé ma carrière suffisamment remplie. J'ai échappé pour toujours à la pauvreté, à la calomnie, aux tempêtes, au spectacle des douleurs d'autrui. Aucun des maux qui effrayent les hommes ne peut plus désormais m'atteindre, et vous me plaignez! Je suis pure et inaltérable comme une particule de lumière, et vous me rappelez dans la nuit de la vie!

> (Virginie is happy now. Oh! If she could only talk to you from the realm of the angels, she would tell you, as if in her farewell: 'O Paul! Life is nothing but a test. I have been deemed faithful to the laws of nature, of love and of virtue [...] Heaven has considered my vocation on earth to have been fulfilled. I have forever escaped poverty, calumny, storms, the sight of others suffering. None of the evils which frighten man will ever be able to affect me, and you pity me! I am pure and unchanging like a particle of light, and you call me back into the night of life!)

Only in an absence from or a transcendence of the world can the ideal of a world rid of unhappiness be achieved. But even in this celestial realm of the angels, the laws which Virginie congratulates herself on obeying are not overtly religious, but those explored by Enlightenment thinkers and writers: the laws of nature and those of love precede those of virtue. Equally, the vices she has escaped are those that preoccupy eighteenth-century writers motivated by compassion rather than notions of dogma: poverty, calumny, storms, the sight of others suffering. Perhaps a little irony also finds its way into her speech since it is clear elsewhere in the text that, had she remained poor, there would have been fewer difficulties.

Virginie's sacrificial death is characteristic of the fate undergone by many eighteenth-century fictional women who are seen at

once as custodians of virtue and victims of misfortune. Here, of
course, her vision is conjured, her advice mediated, by the 'vieillard', a man as wise as 'la vieille' in *Candide* is ugly. Women remain
in a large part the product of man's fears and desires, a character
in his narratives. Yet it is through the agency and in the company
of women that men define themselves. As Rousseau advises in *La
Lettre à d'Alembert sur les spectacles*: 'Voulez-vous donc connaître les
hommes? Étudiez les femmes.' (So you want to know about men?
Study women). The symbiosis of man and woman in French culture remains delicately poised throughout the century, and,
although *salon* culture ensured a cooperation unique in Europe, it
could not eliminate a mutual distrust in many circles.

If, then, happiness on earth is blocked by a society that does not
recognise the qualities and needs of the female character, Virginie,
like Rousseau's heroine Julie, also falls victim to an internal schism.
This internalisation of the obstacle to truth or happiness is characteristic of an age in which the self becomes irremediably
complicated, its capacity for virtue and happiness increasingly
restricted. Madame de Pompadour, Louis XV's mistress, famously
and insouciantly predicted 'Après nous le déluge'. The deluge
which claims Rousseau's Julie and later Virginie is responsible
beforehand for a fundamental change in sensibilities.

Aided by the experience or the memory of the Revolution and
Napoleon, the immediate posterity perhaps prefers to privilege
among the attributes of eighteenth-century French writing the
sense its authors have of the fundamental difficulty and fragility of
human existence and its insufficiencies. When reading eighteenth-
century writers, we then encounter, alongside an unusually
pronounced desire to address and change contemporary matters,
a consciousness of the profoundly human limitations in which they
are grounded. This dimension in an age not celebrated for its
tragedies has tended to be underestimated in more recent years.
Jean-Paul Sartre called French eighteenth-century literature a 'paradis perdu' (paradise lost) in that, momentarily, so he argued,
writers and readers shared the same values and ideals then. In the
previous century, court patronage had meant the author was
always indebted to, but estranged from, an audience, while nineteenth-century authors would be increasingly detached by an

ironic distance from the majority of their readers. We have indeed seen how the writer is variously a hero in eighteenth-century French culture. Voltaire's energy, Figaro's verve, Chénier's passion, all celebrate the saving capacity of the pen to affect man and to effect change. But the strokes of the pen moved so passionately by Madame de Graffigny's Zilia, by Rousseau's Julie and by Rousseau himself, inscribe a change in the status of writing itself, as a resource becomes a compulsion.

Eighteenth-century authors write then not only in order to act but in order to think, to feel, in fact to write. They write not only to effect change but to acknowledge its difficulty. At its most adventurous, an insatiable energy and productivity characterises eighteenth-century French writing, but the voluminous production of writers also betrays a sense that their enterprises are interminable. As soon as many eighteenth-century writers found or acquired what they sought, they realised that the search itself gave impetus and meaning. As the century's explorers ventured ever further into the outer world of experience, so the inner world seemed to recede and stretch out as a new and unknown continent. Many writers try to synthesise these aspects of human experience in a world that seems to change either too quickly or too slowly. Figaro remarks wistfully 'amour sans repos ou repos sans amour' (love without rest or rest without love). This dilemma is inflated into the more serious polarity in *Candide* which confronts us with a choice of the 'convulsions de l'inquiétude' (convulsions of anxiety) and the 'léthargie de l'ennui' (lethargy of ennui). These opposing characteristics find themselves represented respectively in the furious, perpetual motions of Sade's oeuvre and the languorous introspection of Rousseau's *Rêveries du promeneur solitaire* or, embodied by the same work, in the hesitation between lyricism and engagement in Chénier's late poems.

Thus the legacy of eighteenth-century French literature is dual. While the apothecary Homais, among the bottles and labels with which experience is contained, cites Voltaire and preens himself with rationalism, Emma Bovary reads *Paul et Virginie* and looks dreamily out of the window. Eighteenth-century writers speak as persuasively to unhappy women as to successful men.

The search for the truths of the inner world tempts many

writers on journeys beyond language itself. D'Alembert complains about the tedious 'anatomie de l'âme' which tries to bring Enlightenment methods to bear on that which lies mysteriously beyond its capabilities. But in the *Rêveries*, Rousseau speaks figuratively of applying 'le baromètre à mon âme' (the barometer to my soul) in a daily attempt to gauge his feelings, while Diderot in *Les Bijoux indiscrets* gets the female body itself to talk thanks, less scientifically, to a magic ring. The Marquise de Merteuil's soul is described as being worn on her face for the benefit of a society needing to believe in the harmony of inner and outer worlds. But Merteuil herself claims, ironically anticipating her fate when society sees her soul, that, 'descendue dans mon coeur, j'y ai étudié celui des autres. J'y ai vu...' (having gone down into my heart, I studied that of the others. There I have seen...). The search for truth, the quest for a repository of goodness beneath or beyond language tempts all the thinkers, but proves as futile as it is irresistible.

The search for enlightenment in the outer world is likewise compelling but seldom conclusive. It takes French writers and many of their characters abroad, to new lands of opportunity. In Voltaire's last *conte*, the *Histoire de Jenni* (1775), a sentimental union across old and new worlds is achieved. In words that are ambitious as they are simple, the last line of the last *conte* voices a confidence that even if there reigns injustice and unreason, it can yet be identified and negated: 'Un sage peut guérir des fous' (a sage may cure madmen). But Voltaire cannot act as a spokesman for the Enlightenment when even those who believe in distinctions of 'sage' and 'fou' resign themselves to the impossibility of reform. Indeed, B calculates more guardedly at the end of Diderot's *Supplément au voyage de Bougainville* that: 'Il y a moins d'inconvénients à être fou avec des fous, qu'à être sage tout seul' (there are fewer disadvantages to being mad among madmen than being wise all on your own). An appropriately thick mist then descends over the speakers.

The old man's words on behalf of the young woman in *Paul et Virginie* then epitomise some of the movements and ideas that can be observed in the century. But his words are typical also in resisting our attempts to typify. Like so many other texts, it has its own voice whose individuality and indeterminacy frequently obstruct the search for Enlightenment. In *Les Liaisons dangereuses* attempts to find a moral conclusion seem unsatisfactory, just as *Candide* teases us by producing and withdrawing successive endings. The *Neveu de Rameau* likewise simply seems to stop rather than come to a conclusion: 'Rira bien qui rira le dernier' (he who laughs last laughs best). If some characters rest on conclusions that we might find unsatisfactory, even they at length seem to desist. The first-person narrator of Dominique-Vivant Denon's short tale, *Point de Lendemain* (1777), avows in its last words:

Je cherchai bien la morale de toute cette aventure, et... je n'en trouvai point.

(I sought hard the moral of this whole adventure, and... I did not find one at all.)

This story, like the century which it epitomises, has simply ended with one massive shrug of the shoulders.

Glossary

Literary Figures

Alembert, Jean le Rond d' (1717-83): Gifted mathematician and geometer who co-edited the *Encyclopédie* with Diderot, wrote the 'Discours préliminaire' for it and, as Permanent Secretary of the Académie française, championed the causes of the *philosophes*.

Anquetil-Duperron, Abraham-Hyacinthe (1731-1805): Orientalist who collected, edited and translated many manuscripts which he gave to the Bibliothèque du Roi.

Argens, Jean-Baptiste le Boyer, marquis d' (1704-71): Author of the *Lettres juives* (1736), *Lettres cabbalistiques* (1737), *Lettres chinoises* (1739-40), *La Philosophie du bon sens* (1737) among other works.

Argenson, René-Louis de Voyer, marquis d' (1694-1757): Political theorist and author of a *Journal*. Brother of Marc-Pierre (1696-1764), the War minister and founder of the École militaire, to whom the *Encyclopédie* was dedicated.

Babeuf, François-Noël, known as **Gracchus** (1760-97): French Revolutionary and publicist prominent through his periodical, *Le Tribun du peuple*.

Bachaumont, Louis Petit de (1690-1771): Author of the *Mémoires secrets*, a record of daily life in the arts and politics (1762-87) made by the member of the *salon* of Madame Doublet.

Baculard d'Arnaud, François-Thomas-Marie de (1718-1805): Author of numerous plays and, among other works, a set of novellas called *Les Épreuves du sentiment* (1772-80).

Barnave, Antoine-Pierre-Joseph-Marie (1761-93): Revolutionary politician celebrated for his eloquence whose support of the monarchy led to his execution.

Batteux, Charles, abbé (1713-80): Theorist of the arts, author of *Les Beaux-arts réduits à un même principe* (1746) and the *Cours de belles-lettres* (1747-50).

Bayle, Pierre (1647-1706): Influential pre-Enlightenment figure, famous chiefly for his *Dictionnaire historique et critique* (1697 and 1702).

Beauharnais, Marie-Françoise Mouchard, comtesse de (1738-1813): Hostess of a salon frequented by Mercier and Restif among others.

Beaumarchais, Pierre-Augustin Caron de (1732-99): Playwright famous for *Le Barbier de Séville* (1775), *Le Mariage de Figaro* (1784) and *La Mère coupable* (1792) who founded the 'Société des auteurs dramatiques' (1777) to protect authors rights and published the famous Kehl edition of Voltaire's works.

Beaumont, Christophe de (1703-81): Archbishop of Paris, who, having condemned Rousseau's *Emile* (1762), received a famous public letter from him.

Beauzée, Nicolas (1717-89): *Philosophe* and grammarian who contributed the grammatical articles to the *Encyclopédie*.

Belloy, Dormont de (pseudonym of Pierre-Laurent Buirette) (1727-75): Dramatist who spent time in Russia. Famous for his *Le Siège de Calais* (1765).

Bernard, Pierre-Joseph (1710-75): Poet known as Gentil-Bernard who wrote an *Art d'aimer* (1775).

Bernardin de Saint-Pierre, Jacques-Henri (1737-1814): Widely travelled writer and disciple of Rousseau, famous for *Paul et Virginie*, published in 1788 as volume four of the *Études sur la nature* (1784).

Bernis, François-Joachim de Pierres de (1715-94): Cardinal and Ambassador to Rome who wrote poems and memoirs.

Bonald, Louis vicomte de (1754-1840): Author of the *Théorie du pouvoir politique et religieux* (1796) who abhorred democracy and supported the Restoration in the nineteenth century.

Boucher, François (1703-70): Designer of stage scenery, illustrator of books and well-placed influential painter.

Bougainville, Louis-Antoine, comte de (1729-1811): Explorer who circumnavigated the world and published his *Voyage autour du monde* (1771).

Boulainvilliers, Henri de (1658-1722): Free-thinker whose influential political works were published posthumously. An advocate of aristocratic rather than monarchical power.

Boullée, Étienne-Louis (1728-99): Author of a famous treatise on architecture.

Buffon, Georges-Louis Leclerc, comte de (1707-88): Author of the voluminous *Histoire naturelle générale et particulière* (1749-1804). Prestigious naturalist and scientist.

Casanova de Seingalt, Giacomo (1725-98): Legendary womaniser, Italian who wrote a novel *Icosameron* (1788) and the *Mémoires* (first published in 1826) in French.

Caylus, Claude-Philippe de Tubières, comte de (1692-1765):

Archaeologist and collector interested above all in Classical art but author also of the *Vies d'artistes du XVIIIème siècle*.

Cazotte, Jacques (1719-92): Author of fantastic tales, notably *Le Diable amoureux* (1772).

Challe or **Chasles, Robert** (1659-1720): Author of the highly successful collection of stories, *Les Illustres françaises* (1713), as well of travel accounts and memoirs.

Chamfort, Sébastien-Roch Nicolas (1740-94): Author of the much admired *Maximes, pensées, caractères et anecdotes* (1795).

Chardin, Jean-Baptiste Siméon (1699-1779): Painter of genre scenes who won praise above all for his still lifes.

Charrière, Isabelle de (1740-1805): Known also as Belle de Zuylen, born in Holland and resident from 1771 in Colombier, Switzerland. Author of much fiction, notably the *Lettres de Mistriss Henley* (1784).

Chénier, André (1762-94): Foremost poet of the century whose poems were first published in 1819. Precursor of the Romantics, his works include the *Bucoliques*, the *Élégies* and the *Iambes*.

Chénier, Marie-Joseph (1764-1811): Brother of André. Dramatist and author of, among many other works, the controversial *Charles IX* (1789).

Colardeau, Charles-Pierre (1732-76): Poet and playwright whose imitation of Pope's *Eloisa to Abelard* (1758) was influential.

Condillac, Étienne Bonnot, abbé de (1714-80): *Philosophe*, tutor to Louis XV's grandson, the prince of Parma. Author of the *Traité des sensations* (1754) and the *Cours d'études* (1776-89).

Condorcet, Jean-Antoine-Nicolas, marquis de (1749-94): Mathematician and scientist who was Permanent Secretary of the Académie française. Famous for his *Esquisse d'un tableau historique des progrès de l'esprit humain*, written just before his death, an exposition of progress over the ages.

Crébillon, Claude-Prosper Jolyot de (1707-77): Known as Crébillon *fils*. Author of numerous novels, most famously *Les Égarements du coeur et de l'esprit* (1736-38).

Crébillon, Prosper Jolyot de (1674-1762): Known as Crébillon *père*. Playwright, censor and rival of Voltaire.

Dacier, Anne, née Lefebvre (c.1651-1720): A famous Hellenist, translator and/or editor of Homer and others, advocate of the Ancients in the 'Querelle des Anciens et des Modernes'.

Danton, Georges-Jacques (1759-94): Revolutionary leader and orator who helped found the revolutionary armies.

David, Jacques-Louis (1748-1825): Painter whose work spans different ages, successful both during the Revolution and under Napoleon.

Denon, Dominique-Vivant (1747-1825): Author of the *libertin* work, *Point de lendemain* (1777).

Diderot, Denis (1713-84): Indefatigable writer and *philosophe* who edited the *Encyclopédie* and, in an extremely wide-ranging oeuvre of dialogues, philosophical enquiries, novels and plays, tackled all the questions confronting the Enlightenment. Many of his most provocative and influential works, such as *Le Neveu de Rameau* and *Jacques le fataliste*, were published posthumously.

Du Bos, Jean-Baptiste, abbé (1670-1742): Author of the *Réflexions critiques sur la poésie et la peinture* (1719), Du Bos's influence on later thinkers was considerable.

Du Châtelet, Emilie Le Tonnelier de Breteuil, marquise (1706-49): Not only Voltaire's mistress for many years, but a formidable intellect in her own right. Translated Newton's *Principia* into French.

Duclos, Charles Pinot (1704-72): Historian and novelist, best known now for his discursive work, the *Considérations sur les moeurs de ce siècle* (1750).

Du Deffand, Marie de Vichy, marquise (1697-1780): Presided over a famous *salon* and corresponded for many years with thinkers such as Voltaire and Horace Walpole.

Dufresny, Charles Rivière (1648-1724): Playwright who edited the journal *Le Mercure galant* (1710-13).

Dulaurens, Henri-Joseph Laurens, known as (1719-93): An unfrocked monk who wrote satires and subversive tales.

Du Noyer, Anne-Marguerite, (*c.*1663-1720): Protestant refugee remembered for her *Lettres historiques et galantes* (1713).

Epinay, Louis-Florence d'Esclavelles, Madame d' (1726-83): Well acquainted with philosophical circles and an author herself, notably of the *Conversations d'Emilie* (1775).

Fabre d'Eglantine, Philippe-François-Nazaire (1755-94): Minor playwright who became better known as a great Revolutionary.

Falconet, Étienne-Maurice (1716-91): Major sculptor, notably of the equestrian statue of Peter the Great in St. Petersburg.

Favart, Charles-Simon (1710-92): Dramatist successful above all with opéras-comiques. His works were set to music by Haydn and Mozart.

Fénelon, François de Salignac de la Mothe – (1651-1715): Exiled by Louis XIV, his work *Télémaque (*1693, published 1699) retained an enormous influence throughout the century.

Fontenelle, Bernard Le Bovier de (1657-1757): Not only legendary for narrowly failing to be a centurion, but an important early Enlightenment figure who was a continuing inspiration in philsophical circles.

Fougeret De Monbron, Louis-Charles (1706-61): Author of, among other works, *Le Cosmopolite, ou le citoyen du monde* (1750).

Fragonard, Jean-Honoré (1732-1806): Highly influential painter who enjoyed patronage in intellectual and aristocratic circles.

Frederick the Great (Friedrich II of Prussia) (1712-86): A champion of French culture who wrote widely in French and attracted many French men of letters to Berlin.

Galiani, Ferdinand, abbé (1728-87): A Neapolitan resident in Paris who, a member of *philosophe* circles, wrote in French.

Galland, Antoine (1646-1715): Orientalist famous for his version of *Les Mille et une nuits* (1704-16).

Geoffrin, Marie-Thérèse (1699-1777): Host of a *salon* on the rue Saint-Honoré frequented by figures such as d'Alembert, Hume, Montesquieu and Mozart.

Gouges, Olympe de (pseud. of Marie Gouze) (1748-93): Prolific author of plays and pamphlets and the feminist *Déclaration des droits de la femme et de la citoyenne* (1791).

Graffigny or **Grafigny, Françoise d'Issembourg d'Happoncourt, Madame de** (1695-1758): Author of one of the century's bestsellers, *Lettres d'une Péruvienne* (1747).

Grégoire, Henri, abbé (1750-1831): Revolutionary spokesman for oppressed minorities who pleaded for religious tolerance.

Greuze, Jean-Baptiste (1725-1805): Important painter of morally edifying domestic scenes.

Helvétius, Claude-Adrien (1715-71): A *philosophe*, famous chiefly for his work *De l'esprit* (1758).

Holbach, Paul-Henri Thiry, baron d' (1723-89): Influential *philosophe*, notable chiefly for his materialism and atheism.

Jaucourt, Louis, chevalier de (1704-80): Tireless contributor to the *Encyclopédie* in a wide range of subjects.

La Chaussée, (Pierre-Claude) Nivelle de (1692-1754): Playwright said to have invented the *comédie larmoyante* which depicted touching bourgeois scenes.

Laclos, (Pierre-Antoine-François) Choderlos de (1741-1803): Army engineer famous for his novel *Les Liaisons dangereuses* (1782).

Lafayette, Marie-Joseph, marquis de (1757-1834): Important revolutionary figure revered for fighting in the American War of Independence.

La Hontan, Louis-Armand, baron de (1666-after 1715): Soldier who spent many years in Canada and published memoirs and dialogues which anticipated the themes and styles of later writers.

La Mettrie, Julien Offray de (1709-51): Physician at the court of Frederick the Great whose works advertised atheism and materialism.

La Motte, Antoine Houdar(t) de (1672-1731): Poet and playwright famous for disputing with Madame Dacier as a champion of the *modernes*.

La Tour, Maurice Quentin de (1704-88): Probably the leading portraitist of the age.

Lebrun, Ponce-Denis Ecouchard (1729-1807): Poet who was popular and prestigious in the eighteenth century. Known as Lebrun-Pindare.

Lesage, Alain-René (1668-1747): Novelist and playwright whose masterpiece is the *Histoire de Gil Blas de Santillane* (1715-35).

Lespinasse, Julie de (1732-76): *Salonnière* who engaged with *philosophes* and ministers of state alike.

Louis XIV (reigned 1643-1715): The *roi soleil* at once revered and feared. Famous for his military glory and his patronage of the arts.

Louis XV (reigned 1715-74): Succeeded Louis XIV after the Regency (1715-23). Liked to be known as Louis le Bien-Aimé (Louis the Well-loved), but in practice a monarch sceptical, not without reason, of the *philosophes*.

Louis XVI (reigned 1774-92): Fatally indecisive monarch who fled Paris in 1791 but was stopped in Varennes. Executed on 21st January, 1793.

Mably, Gabriel Bonnot, abbé de (1709-85): Elder brother of Condillac who wrote largely on history and politics and was celebrated for the posthumously published *Des droits et devoirs du citoyen* (1789).

Maistre, Joseph de (1755-1821): Famous as an anti-revolutionary theorist and an opponent of the Enlightenment.

Marat, Jean-Paul (1744-93): Powerful revolutionary figure who enjoyed wide popular appeal. Assassinated by Charlotte Corday.

Marivaux, Pierre Carlet de Chamblain de (1688-1763): Essayist, novelist and playwright, whose novels, *La Vie de Marianne* (1731-42) and *La Paysan parvenu* (1734-35), and many comedies remain popular and provoking.

Marmontel, Jean-François (1723-99): Author and theorist who took an active part in the Enlightenment activities, evoked in his *Mémoires* (1792-94).

Massillon, Jean-Baptiste (1663-1742): Preacher whose orations and sermons managed to win admiration in philosophical circles.

Mercier, Louis-Sébastien (1740-1814): Prolific dramatist now famous for his utopian *L'An 2440* (1770) and the *Tableau de Paris* (1781-89).

Mirabeau, Honoré-Gabriel Riqueti, comte de (1749-91): Exuberant Revolutionary politician, orator and pamphleteer.

Montesquieu, Charles de Secondat, baron de (1689-1755): Historian, novelist and political theorist whose monumental *De l'Esprit des lois* (1748) has been as influential as the *Lettres persanes* (1721) have proved popular.

Palissot de Montenoy, Charles (1730-1814): Playwright and satirist, famous for his attacks on Diderot and Rousseau, among others, in *Les Philosophes* (1760).

Pigalle, Jean-Baptiste (1714-85): Celebrated sculptor whose naturalism was innovative.

Pluche, Noël-Antoine, abbé (1686-1761): Priest who achieved great success with his *Spectacle de la nature* (1732-50).

Pompadour, Antoinete Poisson, marquise de (1721-64): Celebrated mistress of Louis XV popular with and supportive of many artists and certain *philosophes*.

Prévost, Antoine-François, abbé (1697-1763): Novelist famous chiefly for *Manon Lescaut* (1731).

Quesnay, François (1694-1778): Leader of the Physiocrats, an influential group of economic theorists.

Racine, Louis (1692-1763): Youngest son of the great tragedian, Jean Racine (1639-99). Author of much religious poetry.

Rameau, Jean-Philippe (1683-1764): Leading composer of the century as well as an influential theorist in his *Traité de l'harmonie* (1722).

Regnard, Jean-François (1655-1709): Comic playwright busy at the turn of the century. Celebrated chiefly for *Le Légataire universel* (1708).

Restif (or Rétif) de la Bretonne, Nicolas-Edme (1734-1806): Prolific writer of novels, stories and treatises whose wide-ranging oeuvre evokes the life and the struggles, sexual and political, in the later years of the century.

Riccoboni, Marie-Jeanne Laboras de Mézières, Madame (1713-92): Actress whose novels, notably *Lettres de mistriss Fanni Butlerd* (1757) and *Lettres de milady Juliette Catesby* (1759), were successful.

Rivarol, Antoine Rivaroli, comte de (1753-1801): Writer famous principally on account of his *Discours sur l'universalité de la langue française* (1784).

Robespierre, Maximilien (1758-94): Radical revolutionary and rhetorician instrumental in instituting the Terror (September 1793 to July 1794).

Roland, Marie-Jeanne Phlipon, Madame (1754-93): Wife of the minister of the interior in 1792-93, author of fascinating *Mémoires* written in prison before her execution.

Rollin, Charles (1661-1741): Historian concerned with education whose work, especially the *Traité des études* (1726-32) was influential.

Rouget de Lisle, Claude-Joseph (1760-1836): Army officer who wrote the words and music of *La Marseillaise.*

Rousseau, Jean-Baptiste (1671-1741): Successful poet who was exiled for the last thirty years of his life for allegedly publishing defamatory verse.

Rousseau, Jean-Jacques (1712-78): Highly controversial and influential author of political works (*Du contrat social,* 1762), autobiography (the posthumously published *Confessions* and *Rêveries*), educational theories (*Emile,* 1762), the landmark novel *Julie, ou La Nouvelle Héloïse* (1761) and numerous other works which continue to be explored.

Sade, Donatien-Alphonse-François, marquis de (1740-1814): Infamous author of subversive novels, many of which were written in prison. Author also of a study of the novel form, *Idée sur les romans* (published in 1800).

Saint-Just, Louis de (1767-94): Highly effective young protagonist in the Revolution who took a leading part in the violent struggles.

Saint-Martin, Louis-Claude de (1743-1803): Poet and visionary who anticipates the Romantic movement. Known as the 'philosophe inconnu'.

Saint-Pierre, Charles-Irénée Castel, abbé de (1658-1743): Political reformer celebrated for his *Projet de paix perpétuelle* (1713-17).

Saint-Simon, Louis de Rouvroy, duc de (1675-1755): Author of the famous *Mémoires* depicting life at the court of Louis XIV, composed in the 1740s of reflections and notes he had been recording since 1694.

Sedaine, Michel-Jean (1719-97): Librettist and dramatist. Author of the most successful example of the drame, *Le Philosophe sans le savoir* (1765).

Sénac de Meilhan, Gabriel (1736-1803): Author late in his life of many works that reflected upon political and philosophical matters, including *L'Emigré* (1795), a novel about the Revolution.

Staël, Anne-Louise-Germaine-Necker, Madame de (1766-1817): Novelist and essayist who wrote on a wide range of literary and political matters from the late eighteenth century onwards.

Tencin, Claudine-Alexandrine Guérin, marquise de (1681-1749): Founder of a *salon.* Author of *Le Comte de Comminge* (1735).

Turgot, Anne-Robert-Jacques (1727-81): Statesman and economist. Author of the *Discours sur les progrès de l'esprit humain* (1750).

Van Loo, Jean-Baptiste (1684-1745): Brother of Carle (1705-65) and father of Louis-Michel (1707-71), all of whom were successful painters.

Vauvenargues, Luc de Clapiers, marquis de (1715-47): Much regretted and admired author of reflections and maxims who died prematurely from smallpox.

Vergniaud, Pierre-Victurnien (1753-93): One of the Revolution's most magnificent orators. Author of the *Éloge de Mirabeau* (1791).

Volney, Constantin-François de Chasseboeuf, comte de (1757-1820): A figure at the forefront of political and intellectual movements in the Revolutionary years. Author of *Les Ruines, ou méditations sur les révolutions des empires* (1791).

Voltaire (pseud. of François-Marie Arouet) (1694-1778): Author of an immense oeuvre that spans and influenced practically all areas. Famous in the eighteenth century as a playwright, *philosophe*, historian, poet, satirist, correspondent, as well as being the author of *Candide* (1759).

Watteau, Antoine (1684-1721): Painter of subjects from theatrical productions.

Index